YES, I AM

By the same author:

C.T. Studd, Cricketer and Pioneer

Continuous Revival

The Deep Things of God

God Unlimited

The Law of Faith

The Leap of Faith

The Liberating Secret

Once Caught, No Escape (autobiography)

Rees Howells, Intercessor

The Spontaneous You

Touching the Invisible

Who Am I?

YES, I AM

by

NORMAN P. GRUBB

Zerubbabel Press
Blowing Rock, North Carolina
USA

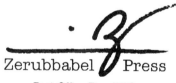

Zerubbabel Press
Post Office Box 1710
Blowing Rock, NC 28605

Copyright © 1982
Norman P. Grubb

First published 1982
Christian Literature Crusade
Fort Washington, Pennsylvania 19034

This printing 2000

ISBN 0-9662957-2-2

All Rights Reserved. No part of this publication may be translated, reproduced, or transmitted in any form or by any means, electronic or mechanical, including photocopy, recording, or any information storage and retrieval system, without permission in writing from the publisher.

Quote on page 20 from *Letters to Malcolm* by C.S. Lewis. Copyrighted material used by permission of Harcourt Brace Jovanovich.

PRINTED IN THE UNITED STATES OF AMERICA

Contents

Foreword to the 2000 Edition	10
Foreword by the author	11
1. Total Truth	16
2. The Son and the Sons	21
3. What is a Person?	26
4. Only Two Alternatives—Which?	29
5. The Necessity of the Negative	32
6. Man's Fall Different from Satan's	37
7. What is God's Wrath?	41
8. Humans Have No Nature	45
9. The Only Two Natures	50
10. We Have Been Deceived about Ourselves	55
11. The Eye-opener about Our True Selves	60
12. The Last Adam	65
13. The First Stage of Restoration: The Precious Blood	69
14. The One and Only Key Turned in the Lock	72
15. The Final Stage of the Restoration: The Crucified Body	80
16. Free from the Law! License?	87
17. A Change of Husbands	91
18. Romans Seven Puts Me Straight	96
19. My Personal Discovery of Total Truth	101
20. It is the Second Crisis	106
21. How Do I Get This Inner Knowing?	115
22. One, Yet Two—a Paradox	120
23. I Know That I Know	124

24. Union Reality and the Charismatic	130
25. I Get Myself Back	135
26. Yes, I Am	139
27. A Woman and a Man Tell It	142
28. What about Temptation?	150
29. James Explains	155
30. That Soul-Spirit Understanding	163
31. On, Now, to the Third Level	167
32. Paul Moving into the Third Level	171
33. From Disciples to Apostles	178
34. Not Two Powers—Only One	185
35. From Negative to Positive Believing	188
36. Faith in Unlimited Action	194
37. Modern Science Helps	198
38. Speaking the Word of Faith	201
39. How it Affects Our Prayer Life	208
40. A Faith Illustration	212
41. What If It Doesn't Happen	220
42. Difficult People	224
43. Body Healing	228
44. From Spirit Action to Body Action	231
45. On to Intercession	235
46. What is an Intercessor?	239
47. An Example: Personal	242
48. Examples: Two Men of God	248
49. An Intercessor in Marriage	255
50. True Love and Infatuation	258
51. A Letter of Much Insight	264
52. Yes, He Is—I Am	272
Epilogue—This is the Reality	282
Song	292

Special Bible References

This is not a complete list of Bible references or quotations scattered through the book, but these do point to a few of the main passages where some Bible subject or author is looked into at greater length.

		Chapter
Romans 6 to 8	Paul on the liberated self-life	15-19
Men of the Bible	In their second crisis	20
Galatians 2:11-21	Peter's shock at Antioch	24
Letter of James	The solution to doubleness in daily living	29
1st Letter of John	Union with God in its completion	29
Philippians 3:3-14	Paul the Intercessor	32
2 Cor. 12:7-10	Paul's thorn in the flesh	41
Gospel of John	With Jesus as the I Am	52

Foreword to the 2000 Edition

Yes, I Am is the third of Norman Grubb's books to be published by Zerubbabel Press. The book has been out of print, and new copies unavailable, for several years. Those of us fortunate enough to have a copy get by with books falling apart, rubber bands holding the loose pages together. We are blessed that God has given us the opportunity to provide this reprint of *Yes, I Am*.

Zerubbabel Press publishes Norman's books with the goal of preserving his message as he intended. While we have attempted to correct obvious misspellings and inaccuracies in the footnotes, we have not changed unusual spelling, punctuation, and sentence structure found in the original.

The costs of publishing *Yes, I Am* have been underwritten by generous contributions to Zerubbabel, Inc. and its newsmagazine, *The Intercessor*. We know that you, the reader, will receive infinite blessings, as have we, from *Yes, I Am*.

Editorial Staff
Zerubbabel Press

Foreword

It is over forty years since I was led, I believe by the Holy Spirit, to write the first of this series of books on the one reality which has absorbed me all these years: Paul's mystery, now made manifest, of "Christ in you, the hope of glory."

The first book, *The Law of Faith,* was followed by *The Liberating Secret, The Deep Things of God, The Spontaneous You, God Unlimited,* and *Who Am I?* I have had many evidences that the inner truth I've sought to share has, by the revelation of the Holy Spirit, become that same reality in many.

Like a fiddle with one string, I still write about this reality, which I boldly call Total Truth. My "textbook," my authority, has always been solely the Bible, and still is—the Bible inwardly illuminated and made the sole key to life by the Holy Spirit; just as Jesus said, "The words I speak unto you, they are spirit and they are life."

I call this book YES, I AM because I would not write it if it were not, by great grace, a personally experienced reality to me, even as it is to many others of you. For as Jesus said, "We speak what we do know and testify to what we have seen."

I sought in my earlier years, as a missionary in the Congo with C.T. Studd, the key to what I call Total

Living—complete satisfaction, complete enabling—and the Holy Spirit turned that key in the lock for me in a crisis of faith which became, though often with stumbling steps, my inner knowing of this "mystery" word of Paul's.

From that time the inner knowing has increased and stabilized through the years, until I could "teach others also" and was better able to define what Paul, Peter, James, and John explain in their letters. This has been the sole heartbeat of my books.

There *is* a joy unspeakable and full of glory, a peace that passeth understanding, and an all-sufficiency in all things by which we are able to abound unto every good work. Though we are always only the earthen vessels in which "the excellency of the power is of God, and not of us," there *is* a reigning in life by Christ, a bearing of the good fruit of the Spirit, an overcoming in all things. There *is* a self-release from bondage into liberty, an overflowing of the rivers of the Spirit, and a counting and experiencing of temptations and trials as "all joy" instead of miseries to be avoided or endured. Because all is centered in the one Reality, our Lord Jesus Christ—crucified, risen, ascended, who now lives His life in His body members—we experience life as adventure, zest, thrill, and gaiety at the heart of a desperate seriousness. Immersed in meeting the needs of others, travailing in birth until Christ is formed in them as in us, we are privileged to bear about in our bodies the dying of the Lord Jesus, so that "death works in us, but life in you."

If you have already read any of my other books, I would say to you that you will find here a repetition of the great foundational facts of our Total Truth, starting with God Himself. I could not build without a sure foundation. If you will go along with me, I am bold to say that God has now given me many new clarifications. These include some startling even to me, ranging from and including the fall of man, what man's real nature is, and our two-fold redemption: not only through the blood, but also through the body of our Christ. Then, at last, a clarity has come to me on those vital Romans 6 to 8 chapters which I have dug into a thousand times, which I can therefore now more clearly share with others. Finally, I go right on to new clarifications of ourselves as the free men in Christ we've been redeemed to be. So we now can say, in accord with the title of this book, "*Yes, I Am*"— and we are learning to live positively in the perfect love that casts out fear instead of in the bondage of negative believing. We see where temptation becomes adventure. The endless problems and frustrations in life, including personality clashes, are seen to be the necessary negatives by which He, the Positive, can reveal Himself; and we enjoy the process with Him. We move right on to the simplicity and constant use of the "word of faith" in our prayer life, and to the highest of all, the life of intercession, in which we are given a privileged and effective place in meeting the world's needs.

If you have not read any of these books before, please be patient if the first chapters seem rather detached from our own pressing life situations. We shall surely get there, if you will follow through.

I have been wonderfully helped in producing this book. I have a job in deciphering my own scribble, and so several who are linked with us in fellowship in Washington and Alexandria have sacrificed their time to type while I have dictated. For this and other vital help I especially wish to thank Dick and Laurie Hills, Dart Cox, Maggie O'Bannion, Nancy Robinette, Lannelle Campbell, Tony and Bette Ketcham, Kay Krattli, and Sylvia Audi; also my son Daniel, a Ph.D. Professor of English Literature, who gave my manuscript a thorough going-over. And my editor at CLC, Robert Delancy. How wonderful the love of God is when dear ones volunteer their labors for Him in our oneness in Christ. My thanks and love to all of them.

This book has its background in the sixty years since Pauline, my precious wife, and I married and went to the Congo together, to take our share in bringing the gospel to our brother Africans, with her father, C.T. Studd. I give some details of this in the book. Pauline, though now physically weak and unable to get about, lies in bed resting in the Lord. Where should I have been without her through these many years? She is now lovingly cared for by one of our Worldwide Evangelization Crusade family, Susie Wheeler, while my daughter Priscilla cares for me.*

In the course of the book I often refer to my years with the Worldwide Evangelization Crusade founded by C.T. Studd, and the Christian Literature Crusade, born out of it, and my great joy all those years in taking my share in the outreach of the Crusades. More recently, the message God has given me to share in these pages has taken more public form in a magazine called *Union Life,* begun five years ago by Bill Volkman, a lawyer, to whom "Christ in you"

---

*Pauline passed, rejoicing, into the presence of her Lord on September 16, 1981.

became a living reality. Quite a company of us are now linked with its increasing circulation, with many evidences of the seal of the Spirit. Various ones of us share what God has made real to us as we receive invitations to homes, house groups, and churches, both here and abroad.

I am thankful to the Christian Literature Crusade, which in cooperation with the Lutterworth Press in Britain has published all the previous books, and now is producing this one.

Finally, as one who years back translated the New Testament from the King James version, helped by the Greek, into a Congolese language, Bangala, I am used to the King James version and like its accuracy, so my quotations are basically from it. I will, however, capitalize the pronouns for Deity.

My greetings and love in Christ to all who read this. May the Lord refresh and illuminate us by His Word and Spirit.

Norman Grubb

[signature]

Not God first but God only

Chapter One

Total Truth

To say something is total truth is the final word! Yet what else can I say if it is total to me? What follows has settled into me as Total Truth, as I have soaked in the Scriptures, always my final authority, these sixty years, and sought the interpretation by the Spirit and His inner witness. Other interpreters of the Word by the Spirit have been my helpers, both in print and in personal interchange; but always I have sought for and found the final confirmation for myself by the One of whom John writes: He who by His inner anointing "teaches you of all things, and is truth, and is no lie."

I have to start with what in itself is the final word, and it is a staggering word to put in a few sentences; but all the rest of the superstructure which enables me to say "Yes, I am," can only be built on this foundation. The Bible says, "In the beginning God," and in the end, "God . . . all in all" (1 Cor. 15:28), as He will then be known by His universe—but is already known by us through inner seeing (1 Cor. 2:10-12). And, quite simply, if He is finally to be known by His universe as the All in all, He who is unchangeable from everlasting to everlasting has *always* been "The

All in all." And that means what it says. If God is the All in all, then all that exists is a unity of which He is the Center, and everything manifests Him, on one level or another.*

That was what first truly opened my eyes to the One whom I had always thought of as a far-off Person quite apart from His creation, producing a new seeing of Him, who is Spirit, as actually revealed in all created forms, even if they have been distorted from their original harmony. "The beyond in the midst." That was a vast stride for me, for it gave me the "single eye" which Jesus said will fill the body with light. I began to be a "see-*through*-er" to Him rather than a "see-*at*-er," in all that is in His universe, whether man or matter, whether evil or good. And I began to find the poise, calmness, hope and faith there is in such single-seeing.

I see also how all the universe seeks oneness, each individual part with the local object of its desire: as shown by the positive proton and negative electron which, united, form the atom; by the human marriage union of male and female; even by the searchings of individuals after political, national, and international union. All these are shadows and symbols of a desire for oneness with Him—most seeking with ignorance of the One with whom they seek union. But millions of us today are the privileged ones who have found that blessed oneness: Christ the Head and we the body. Jesus' prayer is being answered: "That they all may be one, as Thou, Father, art in Me, and I in Thee, that they also may be one in Us." And this

---

*This is what is known as the "monist" view of reality, not to be confused with pantheism. See second footnote on page 20.

right through to the final consummation we thrillingly await . . . the marriage supper of the Lamb, whose bride, ourselves by grace, "hath made herself ready."

We can know our oneness with Him, for as He is Spirit we also are spirit. Jesus had said to the woman of Samaria, "God is Spirit"; and we too are spirits, for He is called "the Father of spirits." So spirit is self: He the "I am" Spirit, and we created spirits—like Father, like son. As spirit-self, *I know*; Paul said, "What man knows the things of a man, save the spirit of man which is in him?" As spirit-self, *I love;* for God is love, and we too all show love, whether rightly or wrongly applied. And as spirit-self, *I will;* just as He "works all things after the counsel of His own will," so I have my freedom of will. This freedom was the first evidence of Adam being a person, in the Garden of Eden. So to be a created person in the image of the Creator is to be spirit as He is Spirit—He infinite and I finite; and I as spirit have knowledge, love and will. I know, I love, I choose; and my soul and body are the external agents of my choosing spirit.

He who is Spirit is He who is love. By the Scriptures, which reveal Him as love in the giving of His Son that we might have life, we know that His love is total self-giving love. He is the eternal Person-for-others. The reason why He is solely other-loving love rather than self-loving love we will see later. But its unchangeable consequence is that this universe becomes to us a safe and perfectly controlled one when we know that He manifests Himself solely in His other-love activities. We know that other-love can only be harmonious love, in which all that has its source in Him who is love—whether animate or inanimate, on every level of existence from the subatomic upwards—can only operate in "temperature" (Jacob Boehme's term for normality or harmony) when each is "loving" the other; and to this the universe is coming.

But how full of contradiction to this is our present experience! We live in a world where self-love is the basic motivation. It seems we are in an inextricable chaos from which we can find no way out—unless it were possible that all humans so love one another that we put the interests of others before ourselves, a condition which, we know, to the natural man is an unattainable ideal. But—surprise of surprises—the ideal has its reality. We who are born of the Spirit, joined to the Lord in one spirit, *are* loving one another! The eternal kingdom of love is already in evidence for those who have eyes to see it.

The world may point at Christians who don't appear to love one another, but the world-wide brotherhood of those who do love one another is a visible fact today, which can't be suppressed or obliterated; and we are part of it. One of the followers of Francis of Assisi said in those days to some who sought to water down his ways of perfect love: "There is an element in the gospel of Christ so disturbing that the world will forever reject it, but never forget it; and the Church will waver forever between patronage and persecution. Yours is the present, for the world will ridicule or crucify us; but I think the future is ours."* And he was right. That "element" *is* alive in millions today, of whom we are a part; and we are

---

*From *Brother John* by Vida Scudder. Quoted in *Gold Cord* by Amy Carmichael, p. 46.

going to see again in these pages the marvels of the way by which this has become our total reality.

So here we start with our Total: God Himself, in ultimate fact the only Person in the universe. God is Spirit (hence we know Spirit is Person), and God is love (and that means He is other-love). And part of this Total we, the redeemed, have now become in our union with Him.

**C.S. Lewis, in *Letters to Malcolm: Chiefly on Prayer* (Harcourt Brace Jovanovich), chapter 13, makes several statements which distinguish monism from pantheism:

"On the one hand, the man who does not regard God as other than himself cannot be said to have a religion at all. On the other hand, if I think God other than myself in the same way in which my fellow-men, and objects in general, are other than myself, I am beginning to make Him an idol. I am daring to treat His existence as somehow *parallel* to my own. But He is the ground of our being. He is always both within us and over against us. Our reality is so much from His reality as He, moment by moment, projects into us . . . . Arnold speaks of us as 'en-isled' from one another in 'the sea of life.' But we can't be similarly 'en-isled' from God. To be discontinuous from God as I am discontinuous from you would be annihilation . . . .

"We must, no doubt, distinguish this ontological continuity between Creator and creature which is, so to speak, 'given' by the relation between them, from the union of wills which, under Grace, is reached by a life of sanctity. The ontological continuity is, I take it, unchangeable, and exists between God and a reprobate (or a devil) no less than between God and a saint. 'Whither shall I go then from thy presence? If I go down to hell, thou art there also.' . . .

"In Pantheism God is all. But the whole point of creation surely is that He was not content to be all. He intends to be 'all *in all*'" (pp. 67-71).

See also: Ephesians 4:6, Acts 17:28 and Romans 11:36.

Chapter Two

The Son and the Sons

Now we can see that a universal of any kind is invisible and meaningless unless it has its manifested form, for any universal reality can only be known by its manifested form. What is electricity? Who knows? But we can perceive it through one of its manifested forms—light, heat, power. Even the living God, the one ultimate Person in the universe, would remain unmanifested for all time as that Person unless He had from eternity His manifested form, first called The Word, His beloved Son.

Why is He called The Word, this One who "was in the beginning with God and was God"? Because a word is the fixed final form that thought takes; and by that word the thought moves into action. Thought, word, deed. Father, Son, Spirit. So the eternal God, as the living Person, speaks His Word of self-manifestation into visibility in His only begotten Son, and that is why "none but the Son knows the Father, and he to whom the Son reveals Him." That is why those in religious faiths who have not Jesus Christ at their center can never know the living God person to person, as we the redeemed do.

But if the eternal universal One is manifested only

by His only begotten Son "in whom dwells all the fullness of the Godhead bodily," then all further manifestations of Himself will be by His Son. To use a poor human illustration, this is much like the procedure of many a human inventor: to expand and perfect his invention he has his next level of cooperators, sons or executives, who do the developing. Henry Ford produces his first car for the people. His sons and managers reproduce it in further popular models ("forms"), and expand the enterprise as a world-wide Ford Company, applying in detail all the resources and genius of the founder.

So now the Son (and later, marvelously, we discover a parallel in the *sons*) becomes Himself the Word in action, and by Him were all things created. Of what did this active word consist, of which it is said, "In the beginning was the Word, and all things were made by Him"? How did He "speak" this word? Quite simply, Scripture reveals. The first word was "Let there be light"—and there was light. So the word was "Let there be." That was no word of striving effort to obtain something. No, it was having the authority to understand what His Father purposed in love-action and was pressing through by His Son-Agent into further detailed manifestation. So the Son, the Word, makes a declaration of what we now call faith, which was also a command, "Let there be . . . ." The word of faith. This meant that the Father-Spirit, who is the eternal substance, would now come into purposed manifested "forms" of Father-love, channeled into visibility by the Son as His creating Agent. "And there was light."

We are here getting a first glimpse, from the very beginning of the Bible record, of how faith works; in other words, the ease of true praying. The Son (or sons) has (and have) an inner understanding of the love-purposes of the Father. The Son then fulfills His prerogative of being the One who speaks the word—and a word, as we have seen, is a person going into action. He authoritatively says, "Let there be" (that same word which Jesus later told His disciples to use, "Say unto this mountain, *Be* thou removed, and *be* thou cast . . . ."). Faith, as the Scripture says, is substance. "And there was light."

Here is our first glimpse of how a person functions. A spirit-person, by his inner action of spirit-choice, speaks the word, the decisive word of faith, and that is really the Son interpreting the Father's revealed love-purpose; and from the Father through the Son, the Spirit Himself, the Third Person of the Trinity, moves into His creating work. At the creation, "the Spirit of God moved upon the face of the waters" and one by one the six "Let there be's" took visible matter-form.

We have here diverged for a moment to take this opportunity of showing that from the beginning, before the human race was in existence, the only way a spirit-person (which is what we humans are) can function is by that simplest of simple spirit activities—the word of faith.

But now back to Him "in whom are hid all the treasures of wisdom and knowledge." By Him, with His word of faith, we see all things come into being—those six "Let there be's," by which the Father manifested His Godhead in every form of marvelous visible creation with all its beauties, harmonies, perfection—by His Son. Indeed, we hear God's recorded comment: "It is good, . . . it is good, . . . it is good." But the consummation of those eight "Let's" is beyond our conceiving, except that it is revealed as His eternal purpose from before He started the founding of the world. When the eighth "Let" is recorded, it states: "And God said, Let *Us* make man in Our image." The Father, Son, and Spirit converged in Their final summit "Let." For it was the beginning of a vast race of sons . . . created spirits in the image of Him, the Creator-Spirit . . . spirits who were predestined to adoption on the level of sons, to actually be co-sons with co-destiny, co-responsibilities and co-authority. "Fantastic!" our astonished hearts say. It is at such times we fall back on our final authority, the written Word. By what other means could these bold facts be revealed and declared?

So here we move from deity to humanity, to discover how we are lifted to the level of deity, because we are created spirits who can thus totally identify with Him the Spirit, and be His perfect means of Self-manifestation. How could we know what that means and implies if He, the uncreated Deity-Son, had not Himself become fully a human, and exemplified in human living what a normal human being is and how he functions as such? So that John can say, "Because as He is, so are we in this world"— not *ought* to be, but *are*!

Then if at this juncture we now take the big leap into the eternal destiny of the human sons as brother-sons of God with the Son, we are quietly told, "If children, then heirs; heirs of God, and joint-heirs with Christ." We then quite rightly ask, "What is the inheritance?" And the answer comes back, "The Father has appointed the Son as heir of all things," and that must mean the universe. Again fantastic!

And we follow that by asking, "What does it imply, to receive an inheritance?" The simple answer is, "After the first excitement at the news, then comes responsibility!" An heir not only owns, but must manage and develop his inheritance. And God has entrusted His whole universe, in whatever its ultimate mind-boggling developments are, to His Son and sons—ourselves!

Just one thing is obvious. He must know that we are trustworthy; even as Paul caught sight of that when he said, near the end of his life, "I thank Christ Jesus our Lord, who hath enabled me, for that He counted me faithful." And how can we be trustworthy and counted as such by the living God? Obviously, only when we spontaneously are *as He is*. Christ is love, as His Father is love; so we as love are then safe managers of the universe because we shall be for *its* benefit, not it for *us*. We are then safe, spontaneous other-lovers, as are the Father, Son and Spirit. That is what we are by grace—not (as we shall see) *ought* to be, but *are*! Yes, *I am*.

Chapter Three

What is a Person?

So now we have laid our Total Truth foundations according to the revealed Word of God—who He is, who we are, and why we are.

The next stage of our inquiry, then, is equally plain. We must now be sure of *being* who we are, as well as understanding who and why we are. And this is our human history. Not one thing out of place. What appears evil and destructive, and surely mistaken and not planned, is found to be His perfect love-purpose from the beginning and is taking us to our perfection in the only way—and none other is possible—by which we can *be* who we are (that is, as He *is*!) even during our earthly pilgrimage, and in simplicity possess our possessions. But this must be examined, diagnosed, experienced in every perfect detail. We must, as conscious persons, know what this "way of God" is . . . so plainly that we can with total confidence walk in it; even as it was said that Priscilla and Aquila expounded to Apollos "the way of God more perfectly." God could not create us like Himself, as conscious persons, without fairly and squarely explaining to us how a human perfectly functions and enabling us to be that.

The first question we must ask is, "What is a human person?" We have already said, "One who loves and knows, and therefore makes choices." That means we are persons because we can discern between things that differ, and thus make our choices. This is what we call moral consciousness.

So we now come to another Total Truth—that nothing can be known except by its opposite. There could not be light in the first chapter of Genesis without, in verse 2, "darkness upon the face of the deep." This is a fundamental law of manifestation. Light cannot be known except by contrasted darkness, sweet by bitter, hard by soft, truth by lie, and so down all the list. A thing is only to be known as a thing because it has an opposite. So all conscious life is a recognition of opposites, and then their rightful combination, so that one is built on the other and one swallows up the other. You cannot have a soft bed unless the mattress has a hard bedstead which it swallows up. You can't say a final "Yes" to this without first saying a final "No" to that. One has said that all life is the "rhythmic balanced interchange of opposites." Even the positive proton has to make captive the negative electron in order to form the elements.

So this brings us to the fundamental principle of opposites which condition a person. We *know* and we *desire* and, as we are forever confronted by opposites, we *choose*. Knowledge and desire lead us to choice. The "autonomy of our freedom" is what the world today is so busy defending, yet that freedom involves the necessity of making choices. We are free, but we must choose. Freedom is not some vague, windblown thing which floats about anywhere and everywhere.

No, freedom must make choices. It exists to *make* choices, because life is only life by the interrelation of its opposites. Those who have tried to escape to what they conceive as ultimate freedom by some mind-blowing drug only arrive at nothingness. Life consists of making choices. We *have to choose*. But the curious effect is that we are all slaves to our choices! We choose to go to a meeting: we are taken over by the disciplines of that meeting. We choose a profession: we are taken over by the know-how of our profession. Our freedom has become a slavery! But because we freely choose, we enjoy our slavery.

So now we see that *to be a person* means we have desire and knowledge and will. Yes, we must make choices . . . and want always controls will.

Chapter Four

Only Two Alternatives—Which?

This brings us straight to the one and only total choice of our desire and knowledge—which totally controls all lesser choices of life. It is *the* choice between ultimate opposites; and remember, our choice always enslaves us and we become that choice. That one fundamental, total choice is between the only two alternatives a living self can and must make. I am made of love—and to love. I must and do love myself. I must satisfy myself. I must fulfill myself. In what direction—one of only two—shall my love by free choice, in which I become so fixed that I am its slave, take me? It can be by my fulfilling my self-love in self-getting, and "to hell with the interests of others!"; or, by my fulfilling my self-love by self-giving, meeting others' needs, and, if necessary, "going to hell for them." When fixed in one or the other of these two, every lesser choice is but a temporary reflection of my one major fixed choice, to which I am a slave.

The most striking revelation in the Bible, almost incidentally recorded, is that the One Person in the universe, our living God Himself, has made the equivalent of that eternal choice. (Of course there is no such thing in Him as a choice in time, such as we make, but we have to use human terms.) This is when the remark is slipped in twice (in Titus 1:2 and Hebrews 6:18) that *God cannot lie*; not *did* not nor *does* not, but *can* not. For a lie is one obvious form of self-seeking. A liar is seeking his own ends, no matter what the adverse effect on his neighbor. And the Bible says God cannot do that. In other words, He cannot be a self-getter, a self-seeker. Thus there has been that determined choice (to use human terms) by the one conscious Self of the universe. *Of course* there has been—for a self is only a conscious self by confronting the alternatives: truth or lie, self-getting or self-giving. And "cannot" means that a self is only a self by its necessary choice, and this is the fundamental total choice. So we have this marvelous revelation: that the One beyond all knowing, in order to be a manifested self-conscious Self, had to make the fundamental choice and, as it were, made it. This self-loving Being (for we read, "For Thy pleasure we are and were created") is eternally fixed as the self-giving Self of the universe. He is the God for others. His self-enjoyment is in self-giving. As John writes, "Herein is love, not that we loved God, but that He loved us, and sent His Son to be the propitiation for our sins." That alone is the meaning of John's supreme word, "God is love"; and that has its basis in, as it were, an eternal choice that He would not be the alternative, the self-getting God. As that great inner seer Jacob Boehme writes: "There is a cross in the heart of the Deity, not just of Jesus Christ, whereby He has eternally 'died' to being a God for self."

That is why He is the *safe* God of the universe, because He is the Lover-Father and can be nothing else. That is why we can learn to have a *positive* outlook on a world of very negative appearances; for we know those are only temporary surface conditions, like barnacles on a ship, like ripples on the surface of a large, transparent lake; and we become those who live by "seeing through"—now, in this present time, seeing His perfect creation, the kingdom of heaven, shining through the surface disturbances. That is why *the only sin is unbelief,* questioning the kind of person God is. We may say we can't account for this horror or that tragedy, but we must never say, "What kind of a God are You to permit that?" We can only say, if we are not to have a cloud over our spirits: "What You do or determine is always perfect love with a perfect outcome."

And so we see the corollary that, if this universe has its safe foundation in its Lover-Father, it must necessarily also be owned, managed and developed by safe sons—lover-sons. And this is why we are so carefully investigating how we are to be "real persons," experiencing our fixedness as safe lover-sons, and walking confidently in that fixity—now, in this thoroughly unfixed and confused world. And once again, there is a total answer.

Chapter Five

The Necessity of the Negative

The first necessity, then, in the coming into being of the human family in God's own image, predestined to be His sons and co-heirs with His own Son, is that we know and understand what it is to be a person. A person must know how he functions as a person, and with what faculties and capacities, before he can take his place in the scheme of things and fulfill his appointed destiny. Hence the old Greek aphorism, "Know thyself."

So from the beginning, Adam and Eve were in a garden where all things were provided by their Father's love; but until they were confronted with alternatives and had to make an independent choice, they were not yet self-conscious persons. (The nearest parallel we have is a newborn infant who knows nothing except his parents' tender care.) Therefore, there had to be in the middle of the garden the two trees with the special instruction given concerning one of them: "Everything is yours; use freely. But don't eat of this one tree."

But more than merely the existence of the forbidden tree, there was already the serpent (who was one of God's creations), and we are told who he is: "That old serpent, called the Devil, and Satan." So God deliberately planned that man should be confronted by the author of evil in the midst of the garden in which all is called very good. This is our first evidence, which appears later all through Scripture and experience, that Satan, though the enemy, is in fact God's convenient agent, always doing precisely what God determines he should do. That makes a great difference in our attitude toward and our handling of Satan, and of all the situations and people by whom he is operating; for we then start not negatively—looking at his lying, bluffing appearance as independent power—but *positively*, by always recognizing that he is merely God's servant, unwittingly fulfilling God's purposed will in his activities.

So here it is Satan, the false god of self-centeredness, put by God in the garden to be the tempter, who first awakens Eve to the consciousness of the total oppositeness between God and devil, between self-centered self-interest and God-centered other-interest. But the significant first fact is that by no other means than to be enticed to satisfy her own self-interest could Eve be awakened to her own self-potentials. Only when Satan said "Look, God is forbidding you to have something you would really like" was she awakened (and thus all humanity) to the reality of human appetites—with the fruit looking so good to eat, and she forbidden to have it. If she could have had it anyhow, like all other fruits, then she would not have recognized the power of physical appetites; but only when she could not have it, but was tempted to want it, did she suddenly see her physical drives. (The same with all that appears to *our* eyes as so attractive to possess.) She was awakened to a whole range of fascinating observations when she saw something pleasant to look at but which she must not have. And finally, the lying statement that God was withholding from Eve the knowledge of the meaning of life in its variety, awakened her dormant mind to its vast possibilities. She had discovered herself as a person with all the potentialities of personhood with which God had created her—all of such unlimited use as can only be suggested by what man in his fallen condition has discovered and developed. How much more surely awaits us when the sons of God operate in their full potential! It will be, as Paul says, like "life from the dead." Flesh, sight, mind are all marvelous gifts of God. Having been misused, as in "the lust of the flesh, the lust of the eyes, and the pride of life," these gifts are restored to us in all the adventure and delight of their *right* use when we are back again as whole persons in Christ. But again we say, only through the enticement to be self-loving selves could we know ourselves as selves. As Paul says, "O the depths of the riches both of the wisdom and knowledge of God."

Concerning this devil, Satan, who Jesus said was "the father of lies" and John said "sinned from the beginning," we are given two glimpses by prophetic revelation of who he is and why he is the enemy. In Isaiah 14, under the temporary symbol of the King of Babylon, this far greater person of angelic status is shown us in his determination to overthrow God Himself and take His place. In Ezekiel 28, when the prophet is speaking locally of the King of Tyrus, this Lucifer, "son of the morning," is shown in his downfall through love of his own beauty. "Lust of the eyes and pride of life" took him all the way to becoming the god of a kingdom of self-centeredness which should never have been in existence. He is that self for *self* which, we have seen, our God, who is the Self for *others*, cannot be. He is that light in reverse which Jesus spoke of when He said, "If the light which is in you be darkness, how great is that darkness!" He is the one whose label is sin: for John says, "Sin is the transgression of the law," and Satan is the one who first deliberately defied the one law of the universe, our God who is other-love. And if our God of other-love is the light and life of the universe, His opposite, who is self-love, must be darkness and death. Yet he had to be, for nothing can come into existence which is not God's determined will; and we are beginning to see that we can never be reliable sons of God in a world which can only be manifested by opposites *unless* we have been confronted with and involved in the opposites to which God has "died," and have *ourselves* experienced a transformation to the same fixity.

But we must keep it clear that, because there can only be manifested life by the fact of opposites, neither side of a thing is valueless, but each is necessary to the other. We wrongly tend to label outer negatives, such as darkness, hardness, and hate, as evil; but they are not so in themselves. What then *is* the good and evil of which we became conscious through the eating of the forbidden tree? It is not in the outer forms of our existence: neither in material things nor in our created selfhood, neither in our soul emotions nor body appetites. It is purely spirit. The name given to Satan is "the spirit of error." God is "the Spirit of truth." Good is the true God in the universe, evil is the false god. Knowing good and evil, therefore, is knowing either the one or the other in operation in our human form or material surroundings. Evils are but misused forms of good. In that sense, John said not that the world is wicked but, rather, that it "lieth in the wicked one" (1 John 5:19, *Amplified*).

Chapter Six

Man's Fall Different from Satan's

The full purpose of the serpent in the garden was fulfilled when he enticed Eve to the point of direct disobedience, by which she entered by experience into the death condition . . . and was followed, by free choice, by Adam. This was no unexpected fall. God intended it, in the sense that He created the human family knowing for certain that they would fall. The proof of this is in Peter's statement that God foreordained His Son to be the Lamb slain for the sins of the world *before the foundation of the world* (1 Peter 1:19-20). He was the Savior in readiness before there were sinners to be saved!

Let us look at the progression of events during the serpent's temptation of Eve. Eve's first step toward capitulation was her acquiescence to Satan's lie. Rather than simply trusting God, she believed Satan's assertions and came to a decision. However, until she actually ate of the fruit, Satan's control over her extended merely to the desires of her flesh and mind (body and soul), but not yet her spirit. Her true spirit-self was still in living relationship with the Father, for she was still capable of hearing His voice, and only spirit can hear Spirit.

In her spirit-center, where choices are made in the freedom of the will, she could yet have cried out to God, admitted the power of Satan upon her soul-body desires, and her inability to resist. Could He have rescued her? The answer was already there. He would have turned her attention to the fruit of the alternative tree which was within her reach, because the trees were side by side in the midst of the garden. If she had stretched out her hand to take *that* fruit, the Spirit of Christ would have taken her spirit captive (as He does ours when we cry to Him at our new birth) and the self-giving love of God shed abroad in her heart would have drowned out that false, deceptive, self-getting love.

But she did not, and we almost say *could* not, for we again repeat: We who are destined to be sons with the Son have to find out the strength and potentials of our created selfhood. This involves having to find the ultimately fixed condition which only comes by being confronted with the two alternatives, the one swallowing the other up—but only when we've experienced both. This, as we should thankfully see, turns out to be the one safe way for God's vast family of sons. We first must taste the full effects of walking the hell way—with its guilt, deceits, sin, and all those lists of horrors enumerated by Paul in his Romans 1 catalogue. Then, when our blind eyes have been opened (first by law and then by grace), we have had such a fill of these ways of death that, once we find the way of escape, we are never going back to them. That is why we are *safe* sons, because we are *thoroughly disillusioned* sons. We may by temptation visit those old ways when no one is looking, as it were, but we are not living there again, thank you!

A human illustration to this is the fact that in acquiring a profession, or becoming competent in any skill, we always have to learn the wrong way of using our tools and turn from the error before we can become competent in their right use. We call that "know-how." That is the purpose of a training or apprenticeship period. We mean by "competency" that the professional, whether a carpenter, pilot, doctor, or what not, knows by now the mistakes and misuses he must avoid, and so is reliable in his profession. If we call in a plumber over some tap out of order, we don't pay his large bill for a simple turning of the tap but for his competency in knowing *which* tap to turn! In precisely the same way, God has His predestined son-family, reliable and competent, because they have been through their painful period of living their lives the wrong way, but have now found the right way and are competent in it.

But there is one historical reality for which we can all be endlessly thankful, and that is that Adam and Eve's disobedience was not of the same quality as Satan's. We have seen how Satan rebelled against God in a total sense from his central self—his spirit. He intended not just to escape God's notice in disobedience, but to replace God Himself and be a god of the opposite quality, of self-centered self. Eve, on the other hand, was deceived and tricked into a self-gratifying action under the stimulation of her soul and body desires, but not from her total inner self, her spirit. She had no intention or desire to cast God out of her life, but merely, as it were, to do something she should not when He was not looking! Hers was sinning from soul and body influences and not from the central self. So she was within reach of the Father and, though a *captive* of Satan, was not like a *son* of Satan. Indeed, fallen men are called "children" of the devil, but never "sons"—though they may ultimately become that by free choice. And that is why, thank God, all members of the human race not only *are* guilty but, hide it how they may, *know* they are guilty, convinced by that light in their spirits which still lights every man. We all know we should live by brotherly love: all philosophies and political parties have that as their main objective. Thank God that though we don't now know *how* to, we at least know we *ought* to. We love our darkness, but we know there is light.

Chapter Seven

What is God's Wrath?

The effects of the disobedience were the opposite to what the natural guilty world would expect God's reaction to be. We would think God would, in anger and wrath, turn His back on the two. But it was precisely the other way around. It was Adam who hid from God, not God from Adam. Here was God "walking in the garden in the cool of the day" and looking for Adam. But where was Adam? Hidden in the bushes. Nor was God displaying some wrathful retaliation, but only questioning Adam . . . to bring the reality of the disobedience home to him. For when He came face to face with the three, the serpent and Adam and Eve, there was not a word of condemnation or wrath against the two, but only His full curse on Satan. To Adam and Eve everything God said was to clarify to them the "beneficial" consequence which they, thankfully, could not escape—a way of life which always has sorrow at its roots. God said in effect, "Eve, you will have sorrow one way; Adam, you will have sorrow another way." That was all. And of course, the point of the sorrow would be that the whole human race through all its centuries of history would always be inwardly miserable, always knowing they were missing the mark and meaning of life, always seeking a phony happiness which would always escape them . . . and thus, always at the heart of every man, however covered up, is a sense of lostness and a longing for fulfillment. That alone was God's judgment on His disobedient children, a judgment totally for their benefit.

Where then is what we would think of—and what the Bible often refers to—as God's wrath? The answer is that the wrath is *not* in His eternal person, for He is only love. But it *is* in the human race, who all have their being in Him; for always, no matter how apparently apart from Him in their way of life they be, they actually live and move in His being (which was Paul's unique revelation to the men of Athens, in Acts 17).

The consequence must always be that we, in our separation from God in His perfect personhood as love, have all the effects in our persons of our wrong way of living; and those constitute the wrath of God, experienced not in Him but in us. This was well put by Paul in speaking of the effects of certain sins in Romans 1—that we receive in ourselves that recompense of our error which is meet. Quite naturally, to fallen man—seeing only with the external eye—it appears as though God is the *God of wrath* imposing punishment on us; and it is good in our blindness that we do see it as that, for then the fear of the Lord is the beginning of wisdom. But to continue in that misconception of God as the God of punishment and wrath after we have become His children by grace, and so should know better, leaves so many people who are justified squirming under the misapprehension that God is punishing them or has deserted them. Even when we read the words of Moses or Paul about God hardening Pharaoh's heart—and that God raised him up to show His power through the hardening—we should understand that the hardening was actually in Pharaoh's persistent refusal to respond to Moses' word of the Lord to him; so the hardening was of his own heart and in himself, as one who had his being in God and was misusing his being. That is the truth of God's wrath in His rebellious sons, for as Paul said, the truth concerning Him is that "God has shut them all up in unbelief that He might have *mercy* on all" (Rom. 11:32, margin), not judgment on them.

Actually, what did God give Adam and Eve in that crisis interview? The answer is in what was addressed to the serpent: "You have sown your seed of enmity in My human family, so that they are your children. But I have a seed [one seed, Galatians 3:16] of this woman, My eternal Christ, the Lamb slain from the foundation of the world; and in all who receive Him, that Seed will destroy your seed and crush your head, though wounded by you in the process." That promise was experienced in its truth by Adam and Eve's second son Abel, to whom God first witnessed that he was justified with the offering of a slain lamb, the first symbol of an atoning death as the gateway to life. And Adam and Eve, as they covered themselves in the skins from slain animals, with which God provided them, must have seen this as the first symbol of atonement. So all God gave them, after this first disobedience that separated them and us from Him, was His all-conquering grace. That grace was in the One who, from that first moment, they could and *did* receive by faith, and who freed them from eternal death.

But the necessity still remained—again we say it—that for us to become reliable sons in the love-purposes of the Father throughout eternity, we must drink to its dregs the reality of the opposite—the misuse of the self in self-centeredness. We must so know it to the depth of its wrongness and misery that, once we are wakened from our blindness in seeking to make the false way be the true, our disgust and hate and disillusion are *so total* that, when and if there is a way of escape, we're "not going to go back to that again." In that we have one secure basis for our new "reversed way" of life. Even if we visit the old haunts under the lure of temptation (as it were, when God is not looking), we're *not staying* there. Guilt, shame, repentance, confession bring us shamefacedly back. Thank God, "once bit, twice shy." A competent professional has learned and discarded the wrong way of practicing his trade. And so have we! Once again it is Paul's "O the depth of the wisdom and knowledge of God"—for God foresaw and provided for the necessity of the human race going the death-way and experiencing its vanity before we could confidently tread the life-way. We are *safe* as well as *saved* sons; not one stage in our history is out of place, the negative any more than the positive.

Chapter Eight

Humans Have No Nature

We now come to what I think is the most important section of this Total Truth, because it has been missed in its completeness by nearly the whole of the Bible-believing body of Christ—a bold thing to say, but it seems to me to be the fact. It concerns what we call our human nature, and that is where our problems and entanglements lie. Even if new creatures in Christ with a new nature, we mistakenly think we have an old, scarred nature—we sometimes call it "the flesh"—which persists in being like an albatross around our neck, a constant rival distracting our attention and stumbling us in our walk. It is precisely that which made Paul cry out, "O wretched man that I am, who shall deliver me from the body of this death?" Wretched, yet redeemed!

It seems as if we acquired an old nature through the Fall, and now have a new nature in Christ, and the two remain deadly rivals, dog eating dog—a struggle from which we are never free in this life—the old man-new man syndrome . . . and the best we can hope for is a means of the new counteracting the old; and yet with a sense that the old always remains in us, though we are Christ's—remains as a deadly element which

Jeremiah calls "the heart deceitful above all things and desperately wicked."

By "nature" we're not now meaning our natural faculties and capacities of body and soul. Our nature, in that sense, means the type of person we are, which is expressed through our soul and body. We may say someone has a kind nature or a harsh nature, a sensitive nature or an unfeeling nature, and so on. But the "old nature" or "new nature" is not the faculties and appetites of a person, but rather the expression of the true personality of the person.

The evangelical church seems divided between two convictions concerning these natures. Each persuasion is antagonistic to the other. One, by far the largest, maintains that we have two natures when redeemed; and we must live with that fact, battling away against the old nature as in Romans 7, and affirming that there is a deliverance in Romans 8 which we must daily apply to relieve us from the pressures of 7!

The other section of the body of believers is strong, persistent, and stoutly convinced that theirs is the truth—though they are in the minority in the whole company of believers and often are considered dangerous or suspect. They are given the general title of "holiness people." They use such terms as "entire sanctification," "perfect love," "full salvation," and are usually considered to be followers of the sanctification teaching that was reestablished in the church through John and Charles Wesley and John Fletcher. There are many precious people among them, with whom I have close links. Their conviction is that after the first stage of our new birth, which centers in justification, we must have a second radical experience of the fullness of salvation in Christ by the elimination of the old man and his total replacement by the new man "created in righteousness and true holiness" with "the heart purified by faith"—and that is the full application of our identification with Christ in His death and resurrection by the Spirit.

Both say we have a human nature. One maintains that our old nature corrupted by the Fall is supplanted by a new nature in Christ, but that the old remains—so that our new way of living is by recognizing the two, the old being counteracted by the new. The other agrees that we all start with a human nature which has become corrupted through the Fall, but holds that the impartation of the new nature in Christ in its totality, by a second work of grace, totally replaces the old nature. The term "eradication" is sometimes used, though most "holiness teachers" regard that as an overstatement of their position, not sufficiently allowing for the continuance of "infirmities."

But *I* am saying that the true revelation of the Bible is that we humans have *no nature*. We're not created to *have* a nature, but to be containers of a "deity nature," a divine nature, and we humans can only ever express the nature of the one within us. All the Bible symbols of our humanity are those of being containers and expressers of one who is not ourselves, but is a god. All that matters is, "Which god?"

The illustrations used of us in our humanity are vessels, branches, body members, slaves, wives, temples. In every case that means we are the agent by which the occupant operates. As vessels, we are said to be either "vessels of wrath" or "vessels of mercy," but we must be either one or the other. The vessel of wrath, of course, is a container of the god by whom we experience *wrath*; and the vessel of mercy of Him by whom we receive *mercy* (Rom. 9:22-23). So it is not the type of vessel that is of importance, but the nature of the liquid that it contains.

The branch illustration is even more explicit, for a branch is but part of a vine, the two being in life-union. A branch is merely the living means by which a vine reproduces itself in its fruit. A branch has no distinct nature; it has the nature of its vine. The fruit is of the vine, not of the branch. And when Jesus said "I am the true vine and you are the branches," He was obviously implying that there is also a false vine producing *its* fruit—one vine being He the true Life, and the other being the usurper (John 15).

We are called temples, and the temple was only the outer means by which the living God manifested His presence. Thus the Shekinah Glory shone through the tabernacle; and His glory is seen in us as His temples. In every case, a temple is only the dwelling place of a deity and reveals *his* presence, not its own. We are either a temple that contains an idol god, or one in which the living God dwells and walks. A temple has no nature but that of the god in it (1 Cor. 8:10 and 2 Cor. 6:16).

We are called married wives, and Paul distinctly says we all in the human race are married to the one husband or the other. According to Romans 7, the moment we recognize that in Christ's death we are cut off from our old husband, Satan, then we are immediately united in a new marriage to Christ who is risen from the dead. No momentary gap between the marriages! And the point is that here he is speaking of marriage in what we might call a biological sense: the wife receives the seed of the husband and bears his children, whether "the motions of sins" or "fruit unto God." The wife is presented as merely the fruit *bearer*, not the fruit *producer*.

Then Paul, in Romans 6:16-23, calls us slaves (as it is in the Greek) and says all of us all the time are either slaves to sin or slaves to righteousness—slaves of Satan or slaves of Jesus. But slaves are merely the property of their owners, with no kind of a life of their own and doing only the work of their owner.

Finally, we are members of the body of Christ, and any body operates by the mind and will of the head, and nothing else. It has no body-led activity of its own.

So in each case the human is only the agent—as temple, manifesting the presence of the deity; as branch, expressing the nature and producing the fruit of the vine; as body member, set in action by the head; as slave, doing the will of the owner; as wife, bearing the children of the husband; and as vessel, only a container and nothing else.

Chapter Nine

The Only Two Natures

Now after this Biblical revelation of what we humans are—containers and agents—we find the Bible distinctly says that we have no nature of our own but express the nature of the particular deity indwelling us. On the one hand, Paul says in Ephesians 2 that while we were in our unredeemed condition, dead in trespasses and sins, we "walked according to the course of this world, according to the prince of the power of the air, the spirit that now works in the children of disobedience . . . and were by nature children of wrath"—not some nature of our own but of our satanic parent, his children in his wrath nature. Then on the other hand, regarding the redeemed, Peter tells us that by receiving "exceeding great and precious promises" we become "partakers of the divine nature." Quite obviously then, it's not some human nature, but God expressing His nature by us. Here are the two deity natures expressed in our humanity.

This could not be more explicit than it is in the Biblical account about the Garden of Eden. There we are told life and death were symbolized by the eating of the fruit of the trees. The Bible tells us that if Adam and Eve had eaten of the right tree they would have received eternal life. Yet we know that eternal life is not in a fruit but in a Person—in Him who said, "I am the life." Therefore, if eating the right fruit means that into our first parents would have come the person who is eternal life, eating of the wrong fruit means that the false deity, the spirit of error, entered in and they became *his* dwelling place.

Now here is the point, the nitty gritty of the reality. All we redeemed humans recognize, when our eyes have been opened by grace, that we were sinners, were under the power of Satan, did his works, were his children. But do we realize that we actually were *he*, in the sense that humans are always manifesting the deity who expresses himself by us? Did any of us know, while unsaved, that we were Satan walking about in our human forms, or that the redeemed are Christ walking about in their human forms? We should know it now, for we are plainly told this.

I remember the surprise when I first read in 1 John 4:4, "Greater is He that is in you than he that is in the world." I knew that "He in me" was the Holy Spirit, but I suddenly woke up to the fact that there was equally "he in the world" in fallen humans, just as much as the Holy Spirit is in us when redeemed. And two verses later John is saying, "Hereby know we the spirit of truth and the spirit of error." That began to open my eyes, and I began to relate it to the symbol of the fruit of the garden.

Then I became alerted to Jesus' words as He confronted those opposing Him, as recorded in John 8:38-44. "I speak what I have seen with My Father: and you do what you have seen with your father," stated Jesus. As religious Jews they resented that, and indignantly responded, "We're not born of fornication. We have one Father, God." Jesus answered, "If God were your Father, you would love Me." Then He broke the truth wide open and declared outright, "You are of your father the devil, and the lusts of your father you will do." When I read that, my eyes were opened to the second phrase as well as the first. The first says that we humans—all of us who have not yet become children of God by faith in Jesus Christ—have Satan, not God, as our father. But the second phrase especially struck me: "... the lusts of your father you will do." Not that we are doing our own lusts, but the lusts of our father. Then all we are doing as humans is not a product of some supposed *human* fallen nature, but actually *Satan himself* expressing his own lusting nature by us! All we are, therefore, is merely the outer expression of this spirit of error, this god of this world, living his own Satan-form of life by our humanity. That was revolutionary. I had always thought I was fulfilling my own natural desires; but not so, because we have no nature of our own. We have all been fulfilling the lusts of the god of self-centeredness, and what we think are just *our* sins are ours only in the sense that we are joined to Satan as branch to false vine, expressing his thoughts and deeds. So when the Bible says "All have sinned," the real inner truth is that the sinner is Satan, and we in a secondary sense are participating in his sinning.

This is the major area in which sin—or Satan, as the Scripture has said—has deceived us; and deceit means making us think that we are what we are not. Satan has played his greatest trick on us in making us think that life is "doing our own thing"—our own self-expression. Who of us in the wide world would ever suspect that we were not just "ourselves" in our self-activity but Satan operating in our form? Of course, Satan himself is the fundamentally deceived one, for he vainly imagines that he made himself independent when he rebelled against God and was cast out of heaven. He imagines himself to be Mr. Independent Self, though actually he is still eternally and totally dependent on his Creator, and doing His will—as we see so clearly in the history of Job.

It is this same false concept of independence with which Satan has infected the human race. We just naturally think we are independent and doing our own thing. Independence is the huge lie swallowed by fallen, blinded, deceived humanity, and the great delusion from which we have to be finally and fully delivered before we can be our true selves. That is what Paul so perfectly explores and aims to deliver us from in Romans, chapters 6 to 8. That is the winning of the final battle over the delusion of the Fall. Our whole life has been built on the false assumption that we are just our own responsible selves, and when changes are needed they are needed in *us*. We can see it in our false self-righteousness, in our fallen days, when we imagined that *we ourselves* were living our own lives of good and evil (which we thought mainly good, with a few evil touches). Actually, all our "good" was evil, for it was a product of the spirit of independent self, the spirit of error. Self-effort *good* is no better than self-effort *evil*, being only Satan's self-effort produced by us. It is one thing to regard ourselves as humans merely influenced by Satan; but quite another matter to realize that it is actually *he* just being himself and living his own quality of life by me . . . and I merely his vessel, branch, slave, temple. I am Satan in my human form.

One reason why the natural man cannot easily accept this fact is that he regards Satan's activity to be mainly the grosser evils like murder, theft, etc. But when our inner eyes are opened, we fully see that the spirit of error, the spirit of self-centeredness, can look highly respectable. We recognize that the self-loving self is usually disguised to make a nice appearance. So, for us who are enlightened, it is not hard to see that fallen humans are Satan—Mr. Self-centeredness himself—in his physical form. It is a profound eye-opener to realize that *all* forms of our apparent self-activity—even if good, helpful, and beneficial to others—are expressions of our self-loving self and thus, in actual fact, expressions of that Satanic spirit of self-centeredness in us. Good deeds are merely a product of the "good" part of the tree of the knowledge of good and evil.

Two other scriptures also brought this into focus for me. First was 2 Corinthians 4:4, which speaks of the lost as those "in whom the god of this world has blinded the minds"; so there he was within us, in our unbelieving condition. The second is 1 John 3:12, in which John exhorts us to love our brothers, and adds, "Not as Cain, who was of that wicked one, and slew his brother." When I read that I asked myself, why are the words "of that wicked one" inserted? Why not just say, "Don't be like wicked Cain who slew his brother"? Because it was *not* "wicked Cain" who was the murderer, it was "that wicked one" who Jesus has said was "a murderer from the beginning," and *he* murdered Abel by Cain's hands. "The lusts of your father you will do."

Chapter Ten

We Have Been Deceived about Ourselves

So we are seeing a tremendous revolutionary reality—that humans never had a nature by themselves. They were both created and later redeemed to express in simple spontaneity and naturalness Him who is God in us and who, Scripture says, "dwells in us and walks in us" (2 Cor. 6:16). Likewise after the Fall, when we had freely joined ourselves to Satan, we had no nature of our own either. So there never has been a "human" nature. Therefore there is no point in considering whether we believers have two natures or one! No, we humans have *none*, but tragically or gloriously, spontaneously manifest the nature of the deity in us.

But as we investigate this actual, factual relationship between God and man—in which man is nothing but the agency by whom God reveals Himself as God, and God in love-action—it becomes obvious that man is not a robot, with no free expression of himself as a person. It is precisely the opposite. We see the total freedom of the Divine Person fulfilling His love-purposes through the total freedom of the human person. And how can that be? It is no paradox when, as we have already seen, freedom must make its choices and the free will then loves to be controlled by its choice. We still do what we want to do. There is no need to force a person's will. All the other person need do is to attract and captivate our "want," and then we will love to act in harmony with him. Give a child another toy, and his crying after the first one disappears. People often ask, How can we conceive of God changing a person's will if he is free? The answer is that God changes our "want," and the will follows spontaneously. Once God has captured our wills by drawing us back to Himself through Christ, then it is He in us who "wills and does of His good pleasure" (and it is always good!) and it is we who naturally, gladly, freely work it out (Phil. 2:13-14).

He who is the "Freedom of the universe" can only be His free Self by His sons as *they* are free. Only with freedom can there be expansion and development, so God's universe can only be entrusted as an inheritance to those free to develop it—to persons, not automata. If there are two freedoms, that of the Creator Person and that of the created persons, the one simple necessity is that the Creator and created be in such a love-union that the sons love to fulfill the will of the Father, and yet always are consciously free in working it out. It still remains an apparent contradiction to reason and logic, I realize, but there is no contradiction in daily living. We who are in this love-union know we are free, and we make our free decisions and carry them out into action, yet we equally laughingly and delightedly know we are doing what is worked in us to will and do. So here is the perfection of freedom which we who have found "the way" delight in, and in which we freely operate.

This revelation from the Scriptures is so central to our very being that we will go over it again, for the repeating of something this important can only help settle the truth more firmly in us.

Our failure to recognize that we Christians are never independent selves and have no human nature of our own but are always, eternally, expressions of the Deity Person whose property we are, and that we manifest His nature, is the root of all our confusion and frustrations. All redeemed sons of God struggle with it in their newly awakened zeal to be the kind of people we know we ought to be. It is the root of our and Paul's Romans 7 "wretchedness." It is the blank wall of obstruction we appear to be confronted with in all of life's problems. It also appears to us as an immovable block in our bringing Christ to others, with their deafened ears or prejudiced hearts. The false concept of independent self is the all-round blockage; indeed, it is the only blockage of all life.

It is the great deception. The serpent deceived Eve; and sin, which is Satan's garment of deception, the Bible says, deceives us. For sin's principle is "I'll do things my way, not God's way"—the precise character of Satan. So what has happened is that Satan has tricked fallen humanity into thinking that we, like himself, are really independent selves, running our own lives in our own way. He has totally blinded us to the fact that we are merely expressions of him, the false deity—actually Satan in our human forms. Who among the millions of us in our lost condition ever thought that we were actually Satan manifesting himself by us? When we responded to the conviction of the Spirit—enough to know we were sinners, under the condemnation of the law, without

God and without hope—we simply saw ourselves as *slaves* of Satan, doing his evil deeds; even *children* of the devil, having his character of self-loving self. But none of us recognized that actually it was he, the spirit of error, who was living *his own life* by us—he being the real sinner and we walking Satans (just as the redeemed become walking Christs). We were under this false conception that it was just *we* who were the sinners, and the sins our own evil deeds, and the self-centeredness our own distorted independent self. And it is because we did not know ourselves as "walking Satans" that we now have great difficulty in knowing ourselves as "walking Christs."

This is what ties us in knots. We have been so grossly deceived—and deceit is much more dangerous than blindness, because when blind we know we are blind, but when deceived we think we are what we are not. We shall be seeing in further detail how this illusion of our being independent selves—and so having certain responsibilities and the particular obligation to be the kind of people we know we ought to be (despite our constant failures)—is precisely what has so distorted our self-outlook. Does it not seem almost blasphemous, or certainly ridiculous and impossible, that we could actually be Christ expressing Himself in our human forms? Look at us! Yes, look at us through the illusion of being independent, responsible people who should somehow become like Him. Now contrast this with the "notion" that we are Christ in our human forms. It is blasphemy! But we will clear this hurdle, and the leap is clear, simple and sane.

So now we have had a first hard look at this revolutionary fact, plain in the Scriptures, yet hidden from (we may say) everybody who is not of the Spirit, and equally hidden from the vast majority of Bible-based believers. It is the fact of the deity-indwelt life being as much the condition of the lost as of the saved. Recognition of this is the key to living with all boldness the liberated human life.

So we will now give time to an examination of how God totally regains His stolen property, the countless millions of free sons who become the "riches of the glory" of His Son's inheritance (Eph. 1:18). We will see again how He had this planned from eternity—the adopted family chosen before the foundation of the world. But it always has been the prime necessity that if they are to be competent, reliable sons by whom He may manage His universe in His own only-way of love-management, then that positive, perfect nature of self-giving love must first be built on the certainty of the swallowing up of their negative nature of self-getting love; for everything is established only by swallowing up or building upon its opposite. And in His eternal wisdom He has always had it planned that the swallowing up would be so complete that the misused negative could never show its head again. The predestined Seed of the woman would tread underfoot and crush the serpent's head, fully removing his infection from His stolen precious sons and restoring them to their perfected sonship.

Chapter Eleven

The Eye-opener about Our True Selves

We shall now turn to the subject of the restoration of us humans to our true being, to the condition in which the Living God, as love, is naturally operative in us and we are "without blame before Him in love," as God originally intended (Eph. 1:4).

The first problem is our blindness. How can that be removed? A basic necessity is to recognize that the whole human family has always had its being in God. We were created in God's image and likeness and are only Satan's stolen property; and for that reason we all instinctively know that we should be living in the likeness of our Creator—people of love as He is, love which fulfills all law. We all know the law inwardly before we come to know it in its outer written form. Genesis tells us that Noah was "a preacher of righteousness" in the years when "the wickedness of man was great upon the earth"—and this before the giving of any written law. Joseph, when tempted to commit adultery with Potiphar's wife, answered her by saying, "How can I do this great wickedness and sin against God?" He, too, knew God's law inwardly.

Glimpses of the reality of eternal law are in the writings of men of history like Lao Tse and Confucius of China; in the Vedas and Upanishads of India; in Buddha's precepts; in Zoroaster and Jalal al-Din of Persia; in Heraclitus, Socrates, and Plato of the Greeks; in Marcus Aurelius, Seneca, and Epictetus of the Romans, and countless others lost in the mists of time. Paul puts it in one word in Romans 1: that all men "know in themselves" what may be known of the invisible God by His visible creation, but "have held down the truth in unrighteousness" and so are without excuse. All the great religions of the world legalistically demand that their followers adhere to certain standards by their own self-effort. This is a total impossibility, for it is in direct contradiction to man's fallen, self-loving nature, the nature of that spirit of error in the children of wrath, "fulfilling the desires of the flesh and of the mind" (Eph. 2:3). So whether it is by Judaism, Islam, Buddhism, Hinduism, or by Marxism or any other secular philosophy of life, we humans who know what we ought to be are more confirmed than ever in our blindness of heart by these self-effort religions and philosophies. We build up our own righteousness and call it the righteousness of God, while in fact it is only this same Satan-indwelt self-loving self producing its convenient good-and-evil fruit of the fallen self.

In Romans 2, Paul mentions both "the law written in our hearts" and God's external, written law given through Moses. What was God's purpose in giving us the Mosaic law? It was to prepare a way by which man's blindness can be removed. In that unfathomable wisdom of His, He uses the pronouncement of an outward law not to falsely establish fallen man in a phony self-righteousness (as though he might keep it—a slave to Satan keeping God's law!) but for a totally opposite purpose. The law was given to expose the deceit of man's self-righteousness, thus stripping him naked of any righteous grounds for standing before God, outside of grace. So the sending of the outer law by Moses was actually part of God's approach of grace to man! Paul's inspired understanding focused Mosaic law to this.

We will follow this through now, both in its preliminary effects on us and to its ultimate completion. This makes Moses the greatest of the law age, to be replaced, as he foretold, by one "like unto himself," yet greater than he, as the son is greater than the servant in the house. The law was given by Moses, but grace and truth came by Jesus Christ.

The outer law, given as a code of ethics on that mount to Moses, was not God coming in fullness of grace to His people, but was inserted as a necessary preliminary. God came to them at Horeb precisely as He eternally is—as the One who rescued them from bondage and brought them out "as on eagles' wings" to be His peculiar treasure. But, even though they were His people, through the Passover and Red Sea deliverance, many of them were like carnal Christians today: they did not know the Lord in their inner consciousness as Moses did. These people, therefore, not yet realizing the exchange of deity in themselves, were wide open to the lying controls of Satan, their former indwelling deity, and thus "carnal, sold unto sin." So to expose their blindness to their Satanic slavery, God added the necessary demand which is the purpose of the outer law. God said to them through Moses that they would be His special people if they would obey His voice and keep His covenant—the very thing they couldn't do, but this they did not know. And so they gaily responded, "Of course we will keep it." They had to respond like that, for this first claim of the law on them was precisely to expose their still unrecognized and therefore uncrucified self-reliance, which was Satan's nature in them.

So the famous law followed on its tablets of stone . . . but significantly it was not given to Moses directly by the Lord Himself on the mount, but by angels (Gal. 3:19), because God Himself is the law lived as person and not in a demanding code with no power given to fulfill it. (It was later, in his second forty days on the mount, when Moses saw God's glory pass by, that the "merciful, gracious, long-suffering, forgiving" nature of the Lord was revealed to him in its full reality—and no wonder his face shone!)

Now the years were to follow in which a few always saw through to grace—many thousands more than the record shows, as we can surmise by the seven thousand who were preserved by God's enabling in the days of dark apostasy under Ahab. If thousands then, maybe tens of thousands in better days. But for Israel in general, sin was now exposed as sin by the law, and it is Paul who brings out the truth that "by the law is the knowledge of sin" and "sin is not imputed where there is no law." Under other dimmer codes, wrong might be recognized as against the doer and society. But only by God's law through Moses did wrong have its total exposure as *sin against God*, leaving man on the eternal death-road unless there be some way back to total alignment with God. Only God's law through Moses makes human wrongdoing totally serious. How significant it is that in these our days, wrongdoing is never acknowledged or confronted as a moral destruction, but only as a social inconvenience or human mistake. No secular nation calls sin by its true name, and that is why the only true light that can still come to our modern world is by the "holy nation," the church of the redeemed who still proclaim the total word of Scripture, and who are the only true nation there is.

Chapter Twelve

The Last Adam

But with the law of exposure comes the grace of restoration . . . the "first Adam" being replaced by the "last Adam" (Rom. 5:12-21, 1 Cor. 15:45). We all have been born in sin and all have committed sin, and the evidence is seen in us all being under the reign of death, with no escape from its sentence of condemnation. Yet this very reality of sin, condemnation and death, making its appearance in the first Adam was—for any who have enlightened eyes to see and who know the character of the Father of Love—the necessary pointing finger to the first Adam's replacement by the last Adam, who would blot out of existence this diseased condition of humanity. He would be the *last* Adam, not just the second Adam—as though the two are on a level with each other and a simple exchange made. He would totally dissolve the death-existence of the first Adam (and thus of us, Adam's earth family) and, as the last Adam, bring into being the ultimate changeless reality of the eternal life-existence of the heavenly family. Where the first Adam was the parent of a human family of "living souls" (selves for self), the last Adam would be the parent of an eternal, unchangeable family of "quickening spirits" (selves giving life to others) (1 Cor. 15:45). And this would be the *last* family, with none ever subsequent to it—for Christ would be "the end of the law for righteousness." So in this sense the first Adam was only the shadow-figure of the last Adam (Rom. 5:14), this bright sun who would swallow up the shadow as if it had never been.

But with one tremendous difference. The whole human race is caught up from birth into the syndrome of sin and death. But the destined coming of the last Adam to transmute our living souls into quickening spirits was not a "had to be." It was a pure product of voluntary love. It only "had to be" in the sense that love by its very self-giving nature is always a debtor, and needs a creditor (which was why Paul the missionary called himself a debtor to the Gentile world). Christ's coming was the spontaneous product of autonomous love, for He is love. So Paul, in this magnificent replacement declaration of the new creation for the old in Romans 5, continually repeats that what we have in our last Adam is "the free gift," "the gift of God," "the gift by grace," "the gift unto justification of life"; and coupled with that, says again and again that all of this has "abounded" to many with "abundance of grace," "grace that did much more abound." Paul was caught by the *glory* of the grace manifested through our "one man Jesus Christ". . . and so are we!

So now we will take the first outward look into the details of this transition . . . which so totally solves the problems which prevent us from being real persons and living the real life we are meant to live.

I know I am writing to those who know the

The Last Adam

historical details of the coming into our space-time world of the Son of God, taking flesh as Son of Man (His favorite name for Himself). He issued from the womb of a virgin mother, with a Holy Spirit father. His early years were under the outer regulations of the law of Moses, during which He profoundly studied, absorbed, and understood the Old Testament Scriptures. His commissioning was at His water baptism, accompanied by the coming of a dove (seen only by Him and John)—and with the dove, the word of confirmation: "Thou art My beloved Son." His acknowledgement of that confirmation that He was the promised Savior, foreseen by the prophets in both His sufferings and glory, was by His public declaration of it in Nazareth. He was established as the unsullied pioneer of the eternal kingdom of Spirit, the kingdom of love—quite different from any earthly kingdom—by his rejecting, during forty days of testing, any self-centered life (Satan's death-life, with which he infected the first Adam). His years of public ministry were of compassionate love combined with manifestations of the power of an unseen world in the visible form of healings, material provisions, counteraction of the force of gravity, and even of physical death itself. These He combined with His ruthless exposure of false, self-exalting presentations of the Living God under the guise of religious practices. He concentrated on training those whom He saw by faith to be His successors, constantly seeing them as what they would be by the coming of the Spirit, in place of their frequent displays of vacillating humanity. By faith He plainly accepted the known prophetic statements about the suffering Messiah, and recognized their truth in the obvious threatening clouds of opposition from the religious authorities which pointed to His coming death. In Gethsemane He took a final agonizing stand of faith: that though He should drink the cup alone, for us, His death would be surely followed by His physical resurrection. By faith—by a declaration which we may call a "word of faith"—He also plainly prefaced His ascension to the Father with a promise to His disciples of "another Comforter," whereby He would make His abode with them in His true Spirit-reality. By faith He commissioned them by the Spirit at Pentecost, and thus equipped them to be Himself... in His many body forms. Through their witness He has entered into millions of further disciples, making them also fellow sons by the Spirit and citizens of a new nation. These now await His personal return and the public joining of Head to body... then the marriage supper of the Lamb, Bridegroom with bride... and finally, His ultimate rendering up of the universal kingdom to the Father, who will then be seen to be what He actually always is to the seeing eye of faith—God the All in all.

All this is a mere repetition of glorious facts known to all of us. But these form the background, in outer fact and history, of what we must now see as *totally applicable to our own inner selves!*

Chapter Thirteen

The First Stage of Restoration: The Precious Blood

We will now see the way by which this combination of the law given by Moses and the grace and truth by Jesus Christ is not only the Total Truth, but the Total Truth to me in my *personal experience*—see how it is the only answer with a totally workable application to every situation, whether mine or other folks'—which makes it possible for me to say to myself, "Yes, *this is it,*" and then declare it to the whole world within my reach.

If this takes further digging into details (with Paul as our guide) to find out the total solution, we will be like a German pastor* wrote:

> God needs *men*, not creatures
> Full of noisy, catchy phrases.
> Dogs he asks for, who their noses
> Deeply thrust into—Today,
> And there scent Eternity.
>
> Should it lie too deeply buried,

---
*A pastor in Hessen, quoted by Karl Barth in his *Epistle to the Romans*, p. 24.

> Then go on, and fiercely burrow,
> Excavate until—Tomorrow.

Some of us have been doing this for years. I could not stop. I must be satisfied. I must have the complete answer. It must be wholly workable in all of life. And we boldly say we have come up with the answer: not our own, but revealed in the Scriptures and confirmed by the Holy Spirit in personal inner revelation.

The law given by God to Moses in its outer written forms, underlining the outer standards of conduct such as the sins of stealing, lying, adultery, murder, malicious destruction of another's character, is obviously intended to produce outer responses. So it does, and for the simple reason that in our blindness we cannot penetrate into sin at its source, but can only recognize its outer products of committed sins. So the first purpose of the Ten Commandments is to pinpoint our guilt before God and produce in us a realization of His wrath, judgment, and our coming condemnation. This it effectively does by awakening in us "the fear of the Lord, which is the beginning of wisdom." Most of us were stirred from slumber by some person or event alerting us to the reality of our condition as lost, guilty, and hopeless sinners—unless there be some means of pardon. At such a time we neither considered nor were concerned about our inner sinful condition, but saw only our sins and their fearful aftermath. Verily, for this was the law established—that by it "all the world may become guilty before God."

Now comes the revelation by Paul of the *first* deliverance stage of the cross of Christ, the amazing but solid replacement of condemnation by justification, as if the sinner had never sinned—the overplus of grace by the shed blood of His crucified body. Paul speaks of Christ Jesus being "set forth" by God on that historic cross as a public, outward demonstration that He had *truly died*. That meant that as the penalty of sin is death, so He who "bore our sins in His own body on the tree" really died, having taken our place in death.

But bodily death is but an outer detail. The real meaning of death is not *body* but *spirit* destiny: Where do I, an immortal spirit, go? If lost, I shall be among "the spirits in prison"; if saved, among "the spirits of just men made perfect," Scripture reveals. So Peter proclaimed in his Pentecost speech (using David's prophecy in Psalm 16) that the Savior went to hell where *we* were destined to go. But hell could not hold Him, for Satan had no hold on Him, and so His "soul was not left in hell." But He could not rescue Himself, for He was there representing us in our lost sinnerhood. He was "raised up from the dead by the glory of the Father."

So through the Lamb's shed blood, death, and pangs of hell, all that should come to us by way of guilt, condemnation, curse, and uncleanness has disappeared forever for all men. "God was, in Christ, reconciling the world unto Himself, not imputing their trespasses unto them." So no man now goes to hell for his *sins*, but only because he has rejected the light of Christ as Savior—the light which has shone into the world. But until the Spirit does His convicting work in us, we love our darkness rather than that light and refuse to come to it.

Chapter Fourteen

The One and Only Key Turned in the Lock

These truths, thank God, are common knowledge to most of those who read this. But it is good to reiterate them, because they are always so precious.

> Upon a life I did not live,
> Upon a death I did not die—
> Another's life, Another's death—
> I stake my whole eternity.

However, we cannot enter into the final, total effects of the death and resurrection of our Christ until we see and share in its two processes, not just one. The first of these is the shedding of His precious blood; the second is the death of His physical body—which we shall look into later. Only by *these two* can this outer law of Moses become what it really is—the inner law of our spontaneous living.

But the key to entering in is *faith*. It is at our new birth that faith first makes its appearance in its true meaning in our lives; but we are, or at least I am, continually deepening my understanding and application of this fundamental principle of living. For *all life is lived by faith* and by no other way. That is why the Bible gives one whole chapter solely to its application—Hebrews 11. So we cannot spend too much time in re-examining it. Did not Jesus say plainly, "If you can believe, all things are possible to him who believes"? And was He not always underlining *faith, faith, faith*? "Where is your faith?" "Your faith has saved you." "I have not seen so great a faith, no, not in Israel."

But we must see first that faith is the only means by which we operate in *all* life—not merely the spiritual, but also the material. Every action taken by man, from the action of the lungs in breathing to the sending of a spaceship to the moon, is nothing but faith in action.

First, something attracts our attention and is desirable. We then also see it is available. Faith is the inner action of our human spirits by which we inwardly decide that we will appropriate or experience this thing. We then speak a "word of faith": "I'll go there," "I'll do that," "I'll take that," "I'll make that." Inner faith then moves into outer action. We go there. We do that. We take that. We make that. Thus faith becomes substance. Faith is replaced by the fact, or rather, *becomes* fact: "I'll go to that home" becomes "I'm in that home." "I'll take that thing" becomes "I have that thing." What was first *desirable* to me, and then *available* to me, now by faith becomes *actual* and *reliable* to me. I experience it. Nothing in heaven or earth can be experienced or become knowingly reliable to me except by the inner and outer action of faith, which turns possibilities into actuality. That is also why all life is really adventure, for *nothing is provable to me until I experience it.* Reason can take me to the outer edge of reality, but I must then leap and take *by faith*. I cannot prove that a chair will hold me and not collapse under me until I sit in it! So we are all "faith gamblers."

Our everyday human experience of faith is what gives us our inner certainties (which we need, for we are inner people). We call this "inner know-how." The know-how then becomes such inner substance to you and me that, when learning a trade, for instance, we boldly adopt its name and call ourselves by it. We learn carpentry and call ourselves a carpenter. We learn medicine and call ourselves a doctor. In actual fact we are cheating! For *what we take, in fact takes us,* whether it is food or chair or profession! The knowledge of medicine or carpentry or cooking or teaching "takes us" as we move in by faith to acquire it, and it becomes our know-how. We then apply our know-how, and call ourselves by its name—doctor, carpenter, cook, teacher.

So we see how fundamentally significant faith is to all life. Life operates only by faith. If this be true in the material realm, then how fundamental faith must also be in the spiritual.

That is why we can never be sustained or "held" by outer religious teaching, or even the Jesus of history—anything which is merely at *outer* contact level. We crave certainty! That is why Jesus told Nicodemus that it was no good, his coming to Him just as a teacher. If he was to see the kingdom of God, he must be born of the Spirit and thus have the Spirit's *inner*-knowing and *inner*-seeing. Paul said that if we are in Christ we are a new creature; therefore we know no man "after the flesh," not even Christ: "Yea, though we have known Christ after the flesh, yet now henceforth know we Him [that way] no more."

Here in the things of the Spirit we use the same faith process as in our daily life. Something is available to me from God's Word . . . something is desirable to me because I see that it will meet my need. But this, of course, is not something tangible or visible which I can take hold of by reaching out my hands to receive it. This is something of the invisible world, something of the Spirit I've reached out for. So how do I now operate my faith? By the same process as in other matters—the *spoken word of faith*. I just inwardly say (and maybe verbally too), "I take this," or "I believe that." For now the substance must come from the Spirit—and as I affirm my taking or believing, the *Spirit* now is what the food or chair was to me in the visible. *He* gives the substance. He does that in my inner spirit-consciousness. He inwardly makes me *know* that I have what I'm seeking. The inner knowing *is* the inner spirit substance. So I operate by faith in the kingdom of Spirit precisely as I do in the kingdom of the flesh, and now faith is replaced in my inner consciousness by "spirit substance"—God-given assurance.

What makes the new birth, which leads us into the substance of the new creation, the greatest event of our human history? Simply because *for the first time* we have been impelled to use our faith-faculty on a spiritual rather than a material level.

At the time of conversion we have become so convinced of our lost condition, through the impact of the outer law, that we are willing to take a revolutionary faith-action. We become aware through the written word—the one material link in the process—of the offer of forgiveness, a removal of all that guilt which propels us to a destiny in hell. And much more, we hear of acceptance by a loving, uncondemning Father who offers the gift of eternal life, purchased by the historic event of His Son's public death on our behalf. And that death, we discover, resulted in a further event which is "beyond human history," His bodily resurrection—attested to by numerous of His disciples; and His unconditional offer to be our Savior requires only that we believe and receive Him as alive from the dead! But that receiving means transferring our faith to the reality of a Person whom we can neither feel, see, nor touch, and who in His resurrection is an absurdity to material-world thinking. This is why it becomes a crisis moment. It is the *absurdity* of faith! Now is the first time we affirm that we are believing in One who was not only crucified—a fact verifiable in history—but who is living, risen from the dead—foolishness to the world, and impossible of material verification! That is why it is the greatest moment in our human history . . . when we, made desperate by our need, are moved by faith into a deliberate relationship with the universal kingdom of Spirit—and with the King of that kingdom.

How does that faith become fact? By an inner spirit-knowing. None on earth can say *how* we know . . . or if we really *do* know! But *we know* that we know. Into us has come an inner awareness, what Paul calls "the Spirit bearing witness with our spirit," that we *are* a child of God. And nothing can shake us.

Our inner eyes have been opened, as Jesus told Nicodemus they would be, to "see the kingdom of

God." And if it is only those born of the Spirit who can see that kingdom, it can be no visible, earthly realm. It is the glorious kingdom of *reality,* for reality is spirit as God is Spirit, and we simply "know" that we are now members of the eternal reality—that realm where Father, Son and Spirit dwell, and we with Them, and where God has all resources, all wisdom, all power, and we with Him. Men now know that this outer universe is only energy or spirit slowed down to visible forms. So we have come home, and are now eternal participators in the resources behind the universe. Never again do we mistake or confuse the trivialities of the "bits and pieces" of material things as being the real and reliable, or irreplaceable. We look, as Paul did, "not at the things which are seen, but the things which are not seen: for the things which are seen are temporal, but the things which are not seen are eternal."

This is now more precious to us than gold that perishes. It is the inner realization, beyond human or rational description, which takes its first living form in the consciousness of the fact that Jesus really *did* love me and shed His blood to take away my sin; that He *is* now my Savior, God now my Father, heaven my home; that eternal life *is* my personal possession. With that blind man put on the spot by the angry Pharisees we say: "One thing I know, that, whereas I was blind, now I see." Spirit-reality is never provable to material sense, including our own soul-senses, so we always appear to walk, as Kierkegaard said, "on sixty-thousand fathoms of water." It is always the "adventure of faith," and we walk by faith, not by sight; but inner consciousness *is* the real stuff of life, and *by that* we *know*—with the outer Scriptures as our bastion of defense and confirmation. But we live because we *know* we know.

This spirit-knowing of the new creation has *two confirming evidences*. One is given the Bible name of "peace." "Being justified by faith, we have peace with God." It is precious indeed, but in its essence it still has a selfish element of satisfying me: I am so glad that I now have peace with God and there is nothing between us. Peace is the first baby-step of assurance given us by God, because as babes we are in a condition in which we have never yet desired anything except for ourselves, so can only be reached by an answer that will satisfy *us*. God's love always reaches out to meet my need at its own level.

But the *true* new-creation reality is neatly packaged inside this gift of peace; for we might not take it were it publicly revealed at the outset. It is the fact of "other-love": that our new relationship is to the living Trinity—Father, Son and Spirit—which is a *Lover-Trinity*. And here is where we are taken unawares. We who have been compulsively *self*-lovers now find we can't help loving the Son who died for us, and the Father who sent Him, and the Spirit who sheds this God-love abroad in our hearts; and this being *other*-love, we equally can't stop wanting to share with others this ultimate reality which is now ours. We become other-lovers. Of course, we do not at first realize that this is not *we* loving (for the human self cannot love in this manner) but that *He* is loving by us. But we do learn that later.

This love is the *one outer evidence* to others that something new has happened to us, because our new out-going love (as well as our peace) obviously affects our daily lives. In that sense, the inner Spirit-awareness which cannot be proved in rational terms is incontestably demonstrated in our lives. Jesus is "seen" in us by others. The True Light has inwardly shone—of which material sunlight is only a rough outer symbol. This new Light becomes to us inner inspiration and ecstasy.

Chapter Fifteen

*The Final Stage of the Restoration:
The Crucified Body*

We now turn our attention to the area of *our daily living*. It has been wonderful to have the disturbing questions of our past and future settled, for, however the world may try to hide it, until we have that settled, it is true of all men that "through fear of death we are all our lifetime subject to bondage." However, we live not in the past or future, but in the present. Have we an answer for its immediate needs? Yes we have, we are boldly asserting, or we would not now be talking it over.

Paul puts it quite simply as he directs our attention from past to present needs. He asks the question, "Shall we continue in sin that grace may abound?" In other words, what about our present condition? Let us get down to brass tacks about our daily lives. Have we a genuine one-hundred-percent life-level which matches the kind of statements scattered throughout the New Testament: "joy unspeakable and full of glory"; "peace that passeth understanding"; "having all sufficiency in all things that we may abound unto every good work"; "reigning in life"; "more than conquerors"; "out of our innermost being flow rivers of living water"; "perfect love"? Or is there only a hit-and-miss attempt at such standards, with more miss than hit? (And we all know there is more miss than hit.)

Paul does not shrink from a face-to-face tackling of such questions. He provides us with both a total answer and the basis for that answer. It is best given in his famous Romans 6-8 chapters, into which I personally have never tired of digging further and further until I have at last come up with what I believe is the right understanding and application of what he is saying. It has taken me a long time to be simple enough to let into my head and heart what Paul is really saying, and not what I might *think* he is saying. The very fact that he adds these chapters to his completed new-birth presentation in chapters 3-5 shows that he realized the matter of full, present "total living" in our new Christ-relationship needed some more thorough examination and explanation—a further turning of the key in the lock—to establish us solidly in Christ as the *new person* we are.

He again hangs his answer round the final completion of the operations of Moses' law on us. He explains how in our new-found sincerity, with a zeal to live consistently (as we should) on totally holy and righteous standards—walking as He walked, loving as He loved—we find ourselves in a struggle between flesh and spirit. We know the law and its commandments; we aspire and we strive; but we largely and disgustingly fail. What we should do, we don't do; and what we hate, we do!

That, as Paul says, is because we have by no means yet been enlightened and experienced the "total exchange" which has taken place in our identification with Christ in His death and resurrection. First of all, we never had it clear about the totality of our former identification with that false deity who had stolen us as his dwelling place—that we were never anything but individual expressions of him, manifesting his nature, not our own. So our present confusion and ineffective living stems right back to that as its source. We have always felt at home with the idea that we are "self-running selves": that we ourselves are responsible for the good and evil in our lives.

Because we were blind to our condition, God in His grace first sent the law through Moses to expose our bondage and reveal to us the nature of the false deity expressing himself through us. In this first exposure, however, we saw no more than the sins we had committed—the breaking of outer laws—and by no means did we penetrate within ourselves to note the sin *nature*—Satan's nature expressed by us. Therefore our first response to the greatness of grace shown in our Lord Jesus Christ was simply to recognize our outer sinfulness, to believe that our guilt and curse had been removed by His shed blood, and to rejoice that God would remember our sins against us no more, as guaranteed by His resurrection.

But what we did not know then (and were not within reach of understanding) was that this was no *real* salvation if it delivered us merely from the outer penalty of our sins but left us as "vessels of wrath"— still containers of the inner *sin-person,* that old serpent the devil, still reproducing his evil fruit by us.

Complete salvation must rid us of producer as well as product, cause as well as effect, sin as well as sins.

This *total salvation*—the totality of Christ's cross-redemption—is the *deeper* discovery which Paul himself didn't see in its full implication until he lived three years in Arabia. This is what he speaks of in his Galatian letter as the gospel which "I neither received of man, nor was I taught it, but [I received it] by the revelation of Jesus Christ." That revelation was centered around not the blood but the physical body of Jesus on the cross. And what is the importance of that? It is because *a living body is the dwelling place of the spirit*, and therefore *when a body dies, the spirit is no longer in it*.

Therefore Paul (when writing to the Corinthians for whom he was an intercessor, and thus having insight into the full meaning of the Savior's intercession for the world) opened up its total significance as no other did. "We are convinced," he in effect wrote in 2 Corinthians 5:14-21, "that when the Savior died on our behalf it was a *body* death, and this means that if He died for all, then we all died." And what did His body represent before God? Paul tells us in verse 21 that "God made Him who knew no sin to be sin for us." Please note: *sin* is not *sins*. By His shed blood He "bore away our sins," but in His crucified body He "was *made sin*." This is fantastically deeper than "bearing our sins," wonderful though that was. "Made sin" is almost unthinkable; for sin is Satan's label, just as we might say love is God's. Satan is, as it were, Mr. Sin, the spirit of error. Where does the spirit of error live? In human bodies, ever since Adam and Eve partook of that forbidden fruit. So when Jesus in His body hung on the cross, "made sin," that body represented all the bodies of humanity, which are all containers of sin. Yes, He *in His body on the cross* was made the representative for all the bodies of the human race having Satan, sin's originator, living within.

There that body died and was buried. When a body dies, the burial is to make it plain that no spirit remains in it. And so it is that Paul can so authoritatively state in Romans 6: " . . . in that He died, He died unto sin once"—not, in this context, died *for* our *sins*, but died *unto sin*. (That is why the blood is not mentioned by Paul after Romans chapter 5. From there onward the subject is His *body death*.) Christ's burial was to signify in plainest terms that no spirit remained in it.

So now Paul just as boldly states that we believers, being *buried with Him*, are "dead to sin"—a truth way beyond being only cleansed from sins. *We are no longer containers of sin* (the same thought as being containers of Satan*), and we are to state this truth and affirm it as completely as we state and affirm that we are justified from our sins. "The body of sin" is "done away with" (Rom. 6:6 *NASV*), meaning that our bodies are no longer sin's dwelling place. And we are to reckon this as *fact* (Rom. 6:11).

Many of us commonly use "reckon" to imply uncertainty. If, with a book in his hand, someone says

---

*Paul, in this chapter and elsewhere, speaks more of *sin* dwelling in us than he does of *Satan*. John and Jesus speak of *Satan*. The reason Paul does this is that he is more concerned with the form by which Satan expresses himself in our daily lives and how we can be rid of that expression. This emphasis on "practicality" is much the same as John shows in his great love passage (1 John 4:7–21): God is love, he states; but then he speaks of how we express love, saying that everyone who loves is born of God, and when we love one another, God is dwelling in us, and so on.

to you "I reckon I have a book in my hand," he is likely implying to you that though he *believes* it is a book, yet he is not absolutely *sure*. Were he sure, he would just say "I have a book." But in the Bible, reckoning means *considering as actual*. To reckon a thing to be so, to count on it as fact, is the first stage of faith that affirms. And "reckoning" will later become "realizing"—which is faith confirmed. But we must start with the reckoning!

But to consider myself *dead to sin* is no light thing, especially when I do not yet appear to experience it. We hesitate to declare "I am dead to sin," because we are thinking about how often sin still seems to turn up in us. But the issue is plain. Will we obey God's Word? In this same chapter, Paul says that we have "obeyed from the heart that form of doctrine which was delivered unto us." Have we, really? So let us "go to it" and be sure we boldly affirm and declare what His Word says we are. Let us not compromise (as many folks do—even teachers of the Bible) and seek to get around this by saying it is our "position" but not yet our "condition"—a lovely little evangelical wriggle. Let us rather obey, and declare what we are told to *recognize, attend to,* and *say*. Then let us go further, after our word of faith and obedience, and find out how this *is* a present fact in condition as well as position.

But if it is a fact that we are *dead to sin,* then it is also a fact that we are "*alive unto God* through our Lord Jesus Christ" (6:11b). As the spirit of error (Jesus "made sin"—2 Cor. 5:21) went out of that representative body when Jesus died, so also the Spirit of truth entered in three days later—and therefore the Spirit has entered *us* through Christ's bodily resurrection. We see the vastness of the implication of that because, for that reason, we who were called the "old man" because of the "old" spirit of sin in us, now are called the "new man" because of the "new" Spirit of the living God in us. The man, our human self, has not changed. But the old indwelling deity, of whom the man was but the expression, has been totally replaced by Another. And thus—with our whole self totally and solely at His disposal—we joyfully recognize our new Owner. Because of *His* new management within us, the old owner, Satan, has no control over us. He can shout at us from without, but he has no further place within. We have changed bosses! We are in the employment of a new Firm!

Chapter Sixteen

Free from the Law! License?

It is at this spot in Romans that Paul inserts a mystifying little statement: "Sin shall not have dominion over you; for you are not under the law, but under grace" (Rom. 6:14). Then the disturbing question: "Shall we [continue in] sin because we are not under the law but under grace?" (vs. 15). Why does he say that?

Paul is going to have further insights to share with us about our final liberation from the law, and our death to it. But before he does this, he wants to make the position finally and completely plain that if we are "dead to sin" under grace, then nothing can get us back to belonging to sin and Satan. As John puts it: "We cannot sin, because we are born of God"—slip into occasional sins maybe, but never again be possessed by the sin spirit and continually express his self-centered nature.

Hence the question: Does freedom from the law, does the magnitude of grace, give me a license to commit sin? No, that *cannot be*; and to present this fact as a kind of Magna Carta of our new freedom, Paul demonstrates it with an illustration familiar to the Romans (vss. 16-23).

"Know ye not that to whom ye yield yourselves servants to obey, his servants ye are, . . . whether of sin unto death, or of obedience unto righteousness?" (6:16). Paul makes it plain that we humans do not have a freedom of our own—that we have no self-operating human nature. We are always servants ("slaves," in the Greek) to one deity or the other. And the deities are here named by their character and lifestyle: sin . . . or righteousness. Yes, *here alone* is our freedom: "Know ye not that to whom ye yield yourselves servants to obey, *his* servants ye are?" *That* is our charter of freedom within slavery: our freedom to belong to *one master only*. And as believers, we have *already* changed our slavery—from sin to righteousness, from Satan to Christ (vss. 17-18)! A slave does not change his owner every hour of the day, or even every month! That is the law of slavery, and of freedom within that slavery. Humans may not always seem so consistently under one or the other owner—we may slip and slither in our outer behavior—but at our spirit-center we're always in *one* of those two slaveries and freedoms (vss. 20-22), fixed and not interchangeable (except by God's grace!) This, then, is how total our transference is from the first Adam's family to the last Adam's, by the radicalness of Christ's once-for-all death to sin and aliveness to God.

This slave-illustration strongly confirms us in knowing in which family and whose service we are— and that our salvation is for keeps, despite any deviations. It equally confirms us into not being hastily judgmental of others in their apparent deviations. See through to the center, where spirit is joined to Spirit! Always contribute faith, not negative downgrading judgment, to any deviators. Our freedom, Paul says, is total freedom from any other claimant. We can never serve two masters, even if we delude ourselves into thinking we can. We were free from God's way of self-giving living while we "enjoyed" the freedom of self-loving living as slaves to sin. But now, through our obedience in believing the gospel truth brought to us (6:17), our service to sin has been severed and replaced by our service to righteousness—which is being servants of God (6:18, 22). We have *exchanged* freedoms and cannot return, and are in the enjoyment of our new slavery!

Then Paul asks, Did you really enjoy that former freedom with its "Dead Sea fruits" of conscious guilt, and the hard labors involved in sinful living? (vs. 21). We had to work for a despot in our inwardly chaotic state of fallen selfhood, and our wages were eternal death! What a freedom!—and how rightly we are now ashamed of it! But our *new* freedom, a free gift, spontaneously produces not works, but the rich fruits of holy living; and the end, everlasting life. Owner "sin" pays wages in eternal death; owner "grace" gives the free gift of eternal life. So here is the royal and wonderful answer to the fear of license some may have because of their new freedom from the law. Is there not danger that, if we're free to do what we like, we'll then choose to indulge ourselves in all kinds of sinning? But the miraculous difference in this new freedom lies in the law of the Spirit replacing the old law. When this truth really dawns, we see it is *not* that it's easier to sin and harder to live rightly . . . but the other way round! It is easy to walk God's way and hard to go back to the devil's ways! It is absurd even to *think* of being the devil's dupes again! What a boldness it gives us when we know that we are totally controlled by the One who owns us, and that we have nothing to do with keeping ourselves. Our Owner is also our Keeper.

How bold it was of Paul—and what a word of revelation—to affirm these two absolute freedoms: If we are slaves of Satan and sin, we are so freed from Christ and righteousness that we cannot change from one to the other. A slave can't free himself. Emancipation can only be accomplished by one who pays the price—by one who buys us back from our captor. So now, freed from that sin-slavery which totally controlled us, we are so totally free as slaves to Christ that sin and Satan cannot get us back again. What confidence that gives us in our own new freedom and the like freedom of our brethren. Paul is going to lead us in chapters 7 and 8 of Romans into the full focus of this truth, so that we shall know with a fixed inner certainty that we humans have no nature of our own by which we might direct our own lives. Rather, we *are* directed . . . and we *are* kept . . . however much, under temptation, we may temporarily wriggle or squirm against our new "bondage" which is our freedom.

So having got that clear once for all—that we are total slaves, eternally fixed to our new owner—Paul can now turn his attention to the one remaining problem which can block our entry into the full freedom that is ours in Christ (and indeed does so until fully and finally cleared away): the control of the law on our deluded independent selves, and the means of freedom from it.

Chapter Seventeen

A Change of Husbands

How wonderful it is!—in our new slavery to Christ we are joyfully free to be producers of the fruit of the Spirit, and cannot come again under the control of our old sin-owner. In our new slavery we say from the heart what it says in that old Church of England prayer: " . . . in whose service is perfect freedom." That is the *fact;* but how about our realization of it?

Let us face it: Though Paul has declared to us the totality of our new freedom as slaves to our new Owner, we often don't seem to have found this fixed level of new freedom working out in our lives, but are caught up again under that old sin-boss. Where does the answer lie? It is in our relationship to the law. We go back to this word of Paul's: "You are not under the law." But in fact we *are* under it and know a lot about the heavy bondage of the law on us with its "you ought" and "you ought not"! Then what does Paul mean when he says that we have full freedom from the law? We must look thoroughly into this and find the solution. For if Paul is saying, "Sin shall not have dominion over you, because you are not under the law but under grace," that evidently means sin *will* have dominion over us as long as the law *does* continue its hold over us. But how to be not only "dead to sin" (6:2) but "dead to the law" (7:4)? And how can that give us our liberty?

Paul explains it like this in Romans 7:1-6. In a marriage, law binds you to your mate. Now we humans started life mated to Satan, expressing his sin nature and producing his children, "the motions of sin in the flesh." But as we have already said, we came into the world *blinded* to the reality of our marriage and to the control of our sin-husband, and to the fact that it was his children which we were producing. We were duped into regarding ourselves as free persons living our own lives. If we had a relationship to sin, it was more as it having some "influence" on us, but by no means having control over us as husband over wife. We recognized Satan neither as husband nor slave-owner over us.

Therefore in our unsaved days, when blind to our true relationship to Satan, God in mercy sent us the law through Moses with its written list of "Thou shalts" and "Thou shalt nots" to shoot holes through our false independence and self-righteousness. We admitted the authority of God's law of right living, for we were still His offspring created in His image. But how husband sin laughed at us: "Fulfill God's law based on being a self-giving self, when you're mated to me, the enemy god of self-loving self? Ridiculous!" He was right. We couldn't and didn't want to fulfill God's law. So God's hidden purpose of grace in sending us the law was first fulfilled not in us humans *keeping* the law (which we couldn't) but in our consistently *breaking* the law, and thus being exposed by the law as guilty lawbreakers, as sinners.

So by the law we were ultimately driven to take

that first great outward step of "coming honest" and acknowledging our guilt, repenting, and being delivered from the curse and condemnation of the law of God's own Son, "set forth" as the propitiation for our sins.

But then comes the further step. The total work of the law is not just to expose the fact of sins committed and the consequent judgment. It is that "by the law is the knowledge of sin"—not *sins*, but the *sin principle* which was dwelling in us when the father and originator of sin dwelt in us.

Paul, through analogy, explains how we are at first married to and totally controlled by our Satan-husband, but then by one stroke the marriage is broken up—Christ's death as our representative cutting us off from the marriage to Satan! Having died with Christ, we are now dead to our old husband. That means that the law can no longer point its finger at us as unable to keep its commands—unable because our husband (who expressed himself by us) would never let us—for death has put an end to that marriage; so the law has no further condemning claim in that respect. "Wherefore, my brethren, you became dead to the law by the body of Christ, that you should be married to another" (7:4).

He then uses the marriage illustration, just as he had used the owner-slave illustration, to bring home the same truth to us: that we humans are always under a deity management. So there's no such thing as we humans remaining unmarried, just the same as we couldn't remain free from slavery. Therefore the marvel of God's grace, says Paul, is that at the moment our old marriage was broken by the death of Christ our representative, immediately in His resurrection He became our new Husband in place of Satan. There's no such thing as a time period in which we are a kind of widow! We have immediately changed husbands and entered into our new marriage contract, in which "the law of the Spirit of life in Christ Jesus has made us free from the law of sin and death" (8:2).

When I inwardly know this and have got the facts in clear focus, I find that my new Husband has me, to my delight, in His total ownership; and I have nothing to do in our family life beyond producing the fruits of our marriage, the fruit of the Spirit. Then the law has disappeared from me, because my new Husband, who is the resurrected Christ, fulfills it by our union life. I thus have become dead to the law in its outer form—the form in which God first sent it, so as to expose me to the reality of my old Satan-husband.

What perfect joy for us who have come this whole way by grace into our new union and know, in its full reality, our marriage to our new Husband! But actually, the point of what Paul is now writing about, and bringing to its climax in Romans 7, is that we've not yet properly understood our relationship to our two husbands. Being all tangled up, our concepts need to be untangled. The tangle is caused by the false idea of myself as an independent person, about which I've been deceived from the Fall. Not knowing that as a sinner I lived under the total management of my old husband and solely expressed him and reproduced his children, but wrongly thinking I then had an independent life of my own, I started out living my new life thinking that now also, as a redeemed human, I have an ability of my own and so can fulfill the law. And so my former husband catches me unaware. When I think I ought to be "doing my own thing" for God (for now, being redeemed, I delight in the law of God) Satan cunningly re-exerts his control over me and causes me to fulfill his flesh will. How can this be? Because "doing my own thing" is Satan's principle, the very cause of his and Adam's fall. It is the sin principle. Here then is the value of the continuing law to my life. I needed to have one final radical exposure of the "nonsense" of my supposed independence. By this, at last, I can see I have never been independent: because the self-relying self was the sin-spirit in me. Until, however, I consciously know and enter into the reality of not only my cutoff from my old husband, but also my marriage to my new Husband, I will still be in an illusory condition of independence, and so actually under the remote control of my old husband. There is no in-between status. So the law completes its work by revealing the illusion of my independence, and grace reveals the reality of my new marriage. Once I move into that, the law ceases to exist as having an outer claim on me, since it is now being *inwardly* fulfilled in me. This is why Paul puts such strong emphasis upon the completion of God's purposes through the law for my freedom, exposing sin as well as sins, and the lie about a time of independence intervening between the old ownership and the new, the old husband and the new.

How wonderful to know that I am now married to Christ! To know that "I am my Beloved's, and His desire is toward me" (S. of S. 7:10).

Chapter Eighteen

Romans Seven Puts Me Straight

Paul then continues to open the truth of the value of the law to us by illustrating it from his own experience, in Romans 7:7-25. It centers around the subtlety of the Ten Commandments, and particularly the one commandment which penetrates through outer acts to inner motive: "Thou shalt not covet." He explains how he was once quite unconscious of any tendency to covet—which he calls "being alive without the law." But later, on some occasion, this tenth commandment hit him. After a first reaction of "Not me—I'm not covetous," he was devastated to find in his heart every form of covetousness—"all manner of concupiscence," he calls it—and this bowled him over. It flooded him like a tidal wave. And so, he states, "sin revived, and I died" to any idea of self-ability to keep God's law. This experience was what God used to open his eyes to the fallacy of self-reliant selfhood and to lead him both into the experience and glorious understanding of "union truth": union with Satan replaced by union with Christ.

So Paul continues his teachings in Romans 7. Let us dig right in and examine in depth what the effects of the law are on us and learn about our final total deliverance from it—which occurs when we've reached the awakened and concerned stage, as Paul did over his temptation to covet.

First, we can clearly identify Paul's "man" as ourselves in our new creation, because "delighting in the law of God after the inward man" (7:22) obviously implies it is someone who has the new-heart outlook of a redeemed son of God.

So here *we* are, inwardly delighting in God's law, and yet frustrated and defeated; challenged by the law, yet laughed at by sin, making it plain that it has us in its control. Here we are, as Paul said, not doing what we should do, and often doing what we hate to do.

But now, through this frustrated condition, maybe sometimes lasting for years, we come to one clear recognition—facts force it upon us: our obvious inability to keep the law. We recognize also that the blame is not on us. We *want* to do the right thing but haven't the power: "To will is present with me, but how to perform that which is good I find not" (7:18)—so at last we can trace the trouble down to the culprit. What a vital revelation! It is not *I*, it is *sin* that dwells in me, *masquerading as self-effort.*

At last, light has begun to break in on us. Twice over (see verses 17 and 20) Paul exclaims, "*That's* it, *that's* it; it is not I, it is *sin* dwelling in me." It is not the redeemed Paul who is the culprit. It is indwelling sin. He sees it plainly to be not himself but something quite apart from himself. "It is no more I that do it, but sin that dwells in me." The culprit is self-relying self! The "sinner" is a separate power who claims to have him as his captive. "I am carnal, sold under sin" (7:14). The commandment came, Paul explains, and when he rose up to do it, sin played a deceitful trick on him: "I've got you. You can't do it. I'm your master and you're my slave, for your very self-reliance is my bondmark in you!"

At that time it would have appeared to Paul, and certainly to multitudes of us, that we are in a condition of permanent warfare. It looks as if we have two natures—my redeemed self that wants to do good, and indwelling sin which defies and defeats me—dog eating dog. And thousands of God's people think that's all it can be: a life of struggle, striving, and much failure . . . with self-condemnation.

And that, of course, is the big lie. But the vital point is that I can't see it as a lie until I first have finally, once for all, got out of my system this delusion that I myself can do good or evil. It is because of this delusion that I either accept guilty failure or put on false self-righteousness. Paul, in that still mistaken idea about himself, had said (7:21), "When I would do good . . . "—but the catch is, a human *can't* do good. That can only be done by Christ in us. And when Paul goes on to say " . . . evil is present with me," he equally can't do evil, for that is Satan in us. But he didn't then know that. Satan alone is the doer of evil; God alone is the doer of good.

But now came the breakthrough of this whole revelation to him—that the human is never anything but the vessel, container, branch, etc., of the indwelling deity. Now he sees it! "The law has nothing to say to *me*. It is not *I* who am covetous; those sinful urges come from an altogether *different* source—not I, but indwelling sin."

The law has really been my friend . . . hanging over me and putting its pressure on me until at last

I see my delusion about self-effort living. Until I see that *self-effort is Satan's principle* the power of indwelling sin has me in its control.

So here is the revelation of total importance—or shall we say, the negative side of the total positive revelation. We can compare it to our prior experience in our unsaved days: I could not settle into the positive recognition of Christ as my substitute and sin-bearer until I first knew, in a total negative way, that I was a lost sinner, with my righteousness as filthy rags ... and nothing I could do about it. Only then could I say, "Oh, I see! *He* took my place."

So now, in this central battle raging around my redeemed self, how can I live my life as a consistent Christian and meet the challenge of the law and its "you oughts"? I cannot see the positive revelation of Christ living His life in me, replacing the false indweller, until I have first seen the total negative revelation of it—that the command has nothing to do with my "human" me except as my being a vessel or container, but has all to do with this false indweller who is still claiming to live in me and express himself through me. I learn that he grabbed me as I was trying to keep the commandments (an expression of self-effort) and "deceived me and slew me." I can now see why it says "deceived me"—because sin was making a whole, lying claim to indwell and control me, while all the time really *Christ* was in me ... and I didn't know it. Until I did know it, and experience it, it meant nothing to me and left sin in deceitful control of me. That was how the law with its "you oughts" also kept its control over me and brought me under its condemnation ... while I was under this lying illusion of self-responsibility and equally in the delusion that sin dwelt in me instead of it really being Christ living in me.

Chapter Nineteen

My Personal Discovery of Total Truth

We have just seen, through Paul in Romans 7, the pivot upon which we turn from frustration and defeat in our newborn lives, coupled with so much guilt and condemnation, to being an "established, strengthened, settled" self. But only in the revelation of Romans 8:1-4 is one able to say with inner certainty, "*Yes, I am*—I am all that I have ever wanted to be: free to be my real self, and to help others to find their true selves." So I will now add my own experience of the necessary preparation for this fresh leap of faith.

I was freed, at the time of my new birth, from the law's condemnation as a sinner; but I thought that I myself, as a redeemed human, still had an obligation to fulfill the law. It was only later that I found I had been totally deceived in this. While, in my redeemed delight in the law, I thought I should be obeying it, Satan kept lyingly claiming his control over me and causing me to fulfill his flesh will.

I had to have one final, radical exposure of the nonsense of my supposed independence. Here is the value of Romans 7:1-6. Through its great light I at last saw I had *never* been independent. I also saw that until I consciously knew and entered into the reality of the cutoff from my old husband and my marriage to the new, I was "in between"—in an illusory condition of independence—and thus actually under the control of my old husband. So the law completed its work by revealing this illusion to me, and grace revealed the reality of my new marriage. As I moved into that, the law ceased to exist as having an outer claim on me and was now being *inwardly* fulfilled in me. This is why (in 7:7-14) Paul puts such emphasis on the fulfilling through the law of God's purposes for our freedom.

So Paul, with that God-inspired analytical mind of his, now "opens up the whole can of worms" about this delusion of the independent self. In 7:15-23, a passage of self-analysis unequaled anywhere, either in the Scriptures or in other writing, Paul shares in detail his own agonizing battle with his personal responses to indwelling sin, and his own total failure to win the battles. There we hear his cry of despair— "O wretched man that I am!" Then comes his blinding flash of revelation that, while he lived in the delusion of being an independent self, indwelling sin falsely claimed to possess him ("I am carnal, sold under sin"). Then the glory of the revelation of the falsity of this delusion, because the One who had cast out the lying usurper has now *replaced* him. So indwelling sin is now replaced by the indwelling Christ!

Thus we arrive at the primary purpose of this great chapter—to show us that death to sin (the theme of Romans 6) includes death to law (7:4). Now we see the boon and blessing of outer law (for Paul defends the law as spiritual, holy, just and good—vs. 12).

God's law, which looks like an enemy condemning me, is really my friend, for it is the ultimate and necessary means of revealing to me that *self-relying self is an illusion.* Having accomplished this, law now ceases to exist for me! "Ye are become dead to the law." How? Why? Because law came into existence only to reveal my slave relationship to Satan and sin and to enlighten my mistaken, deluded self. So now, when at last I know by inner-knowing that in Christ I am totally cut off from sins, from sin, and from its claims on me—and realize that the indweller is Christ Himself, by the Spirit—then I also know that *my inner Christ is the whole law in spontaneous operation,* and I am totally out of range of the outer law. I am dead to it, and it to me. (It may, though, take some time for me, so used to giving ear to an outer law, to turn my deaf ear to it.) Now I live, instead, by the inner leadings—which are also compulsions—of *Him who is love:* and this is the fulfilling of the law (Rom. 13: 10). I now react to any outer claims on me not by a direct response to those claims but by the confirmation of the Spirit, coupled with the Scriptures (which are always a secure undergirding for those inner confirmations). Dead to sin . . . dead to the law . . . the world crucified to me and I to the world . . . I have crucified the flesh in its excessive forms of infatuations and lusts. *That* is the perfect background to my newly liberated life in Christ.

For me this was simplified long ago in Africa—before I took the leap into Galatians 2:20—by one moment of radical and very simple revelation. Still under that old, false idea of being an independent self who could and should be improved as a servant of Christ, I had begun to seek for more love that I might identify myself with my brother Africans. I looked for more faith and power, and more deliverance from the normal pressures of the flesh and critical attitudes towards my fellow workers. The surprise I got, which put me on this right track, came when that simple word "God is love" became new to me. I did not then know that God is all in all, as I do now, and I really thought that God *had* love rather than *is* love, and He could therefore give me a share. But when the Spirit opened my eyes to the fact that God *is* love, then I suddenly saw that love is not some emotion which I might feel and express, but love is a person—in fact *the* Person, when it is *God* who is love. It was as if He was saying to me, "You've got it all wrong. Love is not something I *have* and can pass to you. I *am* that love!" That left me with a question: "Then is there none for me?" And the same query struck me concerning the power for which I was asking—for I became aware of the scripture which says "Christ, the power of God" (1 Cor. 1:24). So power, also, is not a thing but a person—*the* Person—and there is no "special kind" of power which can somehow be *communicated* to us. So again my question: "Well, what about me in my need?"

That conditioned me for the opposite end of this revelation. I saw it by the scripture which says "Christ is all, and in all" (Col. 3:11). "Christ is *all*"—that was staggering enough. But then, "and *in all.*" So I saw that I, as a human, was not to "become something better." I was not to *become*, but to *contain*. That was it! Obviously, if the one I contained was Christ, and He is all, all I needed was to know Him in me as "the all."

That was my first flash of revelation of the Total Truth God has now so widely opened my eyes to—

that we haven't a self-nature to improve or develop. Until then I knew nothing of having been a total Satan-container in my unsaved days, and so knew nothing of now being a total God-container. This was the first revelation of the Spirit (and it *has* to be revealed by the Spirit) that I am just the container. It was the beginning of what has never left me since and has so greatly expanded.

The final illustration that settled me into seeing my proper place as a human was the discovery that several times in the Scriptures we are called "vessels." A vessel is there only to contain. It does not *become* what it contains. The cup does not become the coffee, nor the coffee the cup. That ray of light shot into me. In other words, God was saying, "Stop fussing about your human self, where you fail and where you need improvement. Drop that whole false idea. Vessels don't improve, they just contain. Now turn your attention away from what you are as a vessel—or think you should be. With a single eye, turn your full attention on *Me*, the One the vessel contains." That was enough to move me on to my crisis leap—into the reality of Galatians 2:20, which is now my favorite verse of Scripture: "I am crucified with Christ: nevertheless I live; yet not I, but Christ liveth in me; and the life which I now live in the flesh I live by the faith of the Son of God, who loved me and gave Himself for me." This was my personal experience of Romans 7, leading me into Romans 8.

Chapter Twenty

It is the Second Crisis

Now let us face it. We have seen plainly, from Paul's detailed explanation in his Roman letter, that Christ, our last Adam, completed a total redemption for us, the first Adam's family, in His death, resurrection, and ascension. But it can only become a living fact in our lives by us having a personal inner experience of Him. First there has to be a new birth of the Spirit, and then the Spirit bears witness to our human spirits that we are now the children of God. This witness is vital because we become operative persons in our spirit-selves only by an inner recognition of fact as fact. This is also why Christ's resurrection and ascension had to be confirmed inwardly to His disciples by the coming of the Spirit at Pentecost: it gave them an unshakeable inward confirmation regarding the One whom they'd outwardly seen and touched, but who had now disappeared from their sight. From then on no questions arose, even to the point of their dying for Him whom they knew. For faith was now knowledge. They knew what they knew! Outer facts had inner confirmation, and only by the inner was the outer established.

So now, by our new birth experience, we know

what we know of our salvation and Savior. But we have gone on to recognize that knowing Christ as Savior from past sins must be accompanied by an equally certain knowing of Him as our personal sufficiency for our daily living, and for our sharing of such knowledge with others. Here is a *second stage* of knowing! We have seen in Romans how Paul had to go into great detail, as he moved from chapters 3-5 on to 6-8, to complete for us, as for himself, this second stage of inner knowing. He has made it plain that there are travailings, searchings, negative condemnings and failures to condition us for this second, equally certain, knowing. We have to go through our Romans 7 experience. There's no shortcut for us on our "wilderness way," any more than there was for the children of Israel in their painful sojourn in that "waste and howling wilderness."

So we are now confronting this together. Let's not fool ourselves. We shan't get there any more quickly and easily than Paul (although we may have more head knowledge because of the pioneering route-map he has drawn for us). Any close look at the great biographies of the Bible presents us with the same fact.

Abraham, our father of faith, that total follower of the God of glory who had appeared to him, had many achievements of faith en route. But he did not reach his fixed *inner knowing* until he had been through many years of frustration with Hagar and Sarah and the flesh birth of Ishmael . . . for he was not yet able to discern between the mind of the flesh and the pure word of the Spirit. His fixed inner knowing came by the crisis of faith—faith in the impossible—at the birth of Isaac. After that he could hear ever so plainly, even when later called by God to the further impossible and most ridiculous offering of his son as a burnt sacrifice.

Moses, that dedicated servant of God, had to go beyond his initial commitment, even through a hard forty years at the backside of the desert, before he was fixed in his inner total sufficiency and adequacy at the burning bush. And from then on he *inwardly* knew the One with whom the children of Israel had only an outer relationship of faith.

Jacob, during his years of frustrating service with Laban, had become true-hearted and intense in his pursuit of the living God. But it was only through a final night of struggle (Gen. 32:24-32), in which the angel of the Lord brought him to a physically broken place, with his thigh out of joint, so there could be no running away from his threatening meeting with Esau—only through that experience did he know himself by inner revelation as "a prince who has power with God and man."

Joshua, splendidly gifted as a military leader, had to reach the desperate end of his self-confidence by a near collapse into cowardice, by being one of the twelve spies who brought back such a defeatist report to Moses. That night Joshua "inwardly died" and rose the next morning to side with Moses and Caleb and risk the stoning that threatened them. From then onward he became a man "in whom is the Spirit of God," and Moses' trusted successor.

David, after his youthful nation-stirring triumph of faith over Goliath, and his shepherd years as the sweet psalmist of Israel, had to spend eight years as a fugitive from Saul. While living in caves, he and his band of "the disappointed and disgruntled" were being trained together as God's men, until, at the fiery trial at Ziklag, even his loved men turned on him. There he took a personal stand of faith which brought him into his inner knowing, when he "encouraged himself in the Lord his God" (1 Sam. 30:6).

Elisha, the wealthy young farmer who gladly sold all to follow the Lord with Elijah, spent eight years "pouring water" on the hands of his tough old leader; and even then he had to follow him in persistent pursuit to the moment of his ascent to heaven in a whirlwind, until he could himself inwardly receive and know that double portion of the Spirit which made him the successor of that mighty prophet.

Even the Savior Himself, the Son of God, taking flesh as Son of man, was intently studying the Scriptures all those years in the carpenter's shop, knowing from the Scriptures who He was. But only at His baptism, by the dove and the word of His Father from heaven, did He have the total inner confirmation, which established Him as the one who could declare with Isaiah's prophetic words, "The Spirit of the Lord is upon Me," and "This day is this scripture fulfilled in your ears."

So also Paul did not "know" until his three years in Arabia; and even Peter, though the leader at Pentecost, until confronted by Paul in Antioch (which we shall refer to later in more detail).

Bible biographies give plenty of evidence that we move on from a relationship-knowing at our new birth to a total *inner knowing*. Paul gives us the transforming details in Romans 7 and 8, as we follow him on from his penetrating understanding of the true facts about himself to his agonized cry, "O wretched man that I am! who shall deliver me from the body of this death?" and to his glorious liberated shout of inner recognition in 8:1-2, "Now I see! There is no more self-condemnation, no more beating my head against the brick wall of failure and defeat! I am set free! I *know* I am, and am free forever!" In his own written words, "The law of the Spirit of life in Christ Jesus has set me free from the law of sin and death" (*RSV*)—*has*, not might, may or will. The Spirit was inwardly confirming what Paul had believed as a fact of history—that by Christ's body-death on Calvary, indwelling Satan was out and indwelling Christ was in; and Paul was underlining for us in this shout of victory that he was a liberated person, not only because Jesus had died and risen in history, but also because the Spirit inwardly confirmed it to him. It was the inner confirmation of the Spirit that set him free. No hearing of given facts, not even a reckoning on them, could do this for him; only the actual confirmation within him had finally "fixed him" in who he really was. I am free! I am free! Yes, *I am! I am! I am!*

So whether by sudden crisis—as it was for those Bible men and has been for most of us—or by some other means, no matter what—*we do know*. And we are now going to find out *how* we can know.

Knowing is not mental understanding, or external believing, or reckoning. It is something beyond words, because it is spirit; it is the reality of the spirit realm, beyond natural reasoning. We recognize this already on the new-birth level: How did we come to know we were born of the Spirit? Can you say? Can I? We cannot. Likewise now: we simply say to the outer, inquiring world—and indeed to thousands of church believers, who so often want to know but have never been shown this Biblical way of faith—that we just *inwardly know*.

We can use an example from the human level—that we become competent in our profession only by an inner knowing of it. First we give ourselves to training and study, which is our first step of faith into acquiring this body of knowledge wholly outside us. As we persist in our strivings to attain, somewhere along the line what was beyond our reach just becomes part of us. We know it! We know our stuff, and have moved over from learning to being, and we boldly call ourselves by the name of our competency—doctor, cook, teacher. And we operate not by the outer tools of our trade, but by our inner know-how.

In the same way, in our new birth the Spirit has made us inner-knowers of the outer historic facts of our salvation. Actually, on our new-birth level, the confirmation of the Spirit is usually immediate, or appears so—though in actual fact it was not. We first had our gestation period. It went on maybe for years—the work of the law bringing conviction, honest facing of sin and guilt, repentance, and finally a crisis moment of faith and open confession. But all that could not establish us as *confident* Christians, who know and love to share what we know. The *inner knowing* did that.

So now let us face this. We are about to find out how we enter into this *second* inner knowing. It also comes naturally and effortlessly, and with a certainty that we never lose again. I now know that not only do I have Christ as my Savior from sin, but that I have passed through an inner experience of death to my former striving, sin-dominated, and self-condemning self. I now know that I am dead to sin, the world, flesh-dominion, and law; and now I equally know that I am no longer a lonely, independent "I," or still worse, have sin and Satan living in me. I know that in place of "I" it is now *Christ* living His life in me. And this I now *know*—actually *know*—without ever again having to reckon on it, or trying to reassure myself about it, or refreshing my recognition of it.

This does not mean that we are like two people separate within myself. No, we are one. I am "joined to the Lord—one spirit" (1 Cor. 6:17); we are *two*, yet we are *one*. He is the One living in me, yet not as separate from me, but reproducing Himself by me—as vine through branch, head through body, husband through wife.

In that union relationship I can say that it is *Christ* who is manifested in my human form—just as it is when He says that both He and I are "the light of the world" (John 8:12, Matt. 5:14). In actual fact, we are two—light and lamp, and He is the light shining through the lamp. Yet we so forget the existence of the lamp that when we come into a room we don't say "Turn on the lamp" but "Turn on the light"! So in our conscious union relationship: though each Christian really is the two united in one, we don't see *ourselves* as thinking, speaking, acting, but it is *He expressed through our forms* doing the thinking, speaking and acting.

It was in the glory of this inner consciousness that Paul said, "I am crucified with Christ, nevertheless I live; no, not I, it is *Christ* living in me." That paradoxical contradiction was the only way in which he could describe a union-and-replacement experience in words. "I live in His resurrection life.... No, I must contradict that—it is not I, but Christ living in me." That is the union-duality! We are two, but no, we are one—and so much one that I speak of *His doing the living in place of me*. "Not I, but Christ living in me." That is the nearest in third-dimensional human words that he can put a fourth-dimensional union truth. It is Christ in his Paul form; Christ in even *my* human form. And from the moment that the light of this inner knowing is "turned on" in me, it becomes *real* to my consciousness that it is not *I* thinking, speaking, acting, but it is *He*. And so it is!

Yet all this hangs, in the end, on personal experience . . . and we are now going to find out how we may have this experience. Union is no good being a fact for me unless I know it to be so and thus can "use" it. The fact that in Christ I already was given total deliverance from both sins and sin is meaningless for me until I know it by experience. A carpenter can only use the tools he knows how to use. That was why sin could laugh at me and deceive me during those long years of struggle in my Christian living. I didn't inwardly know I was totally delivered from its indwelling presence, so it continued to mock me with a false claim of dwelling in me. Again I repeat, we are all always controlled by our inner believings . . . which become knowings. All depends on how I am seeing things. When, therefore, I don't know by an inner knowing (even though I might have an outer reckoning) that it is *Christ* living in my human self, and not sin or Satan, then I continue under the delusion of sin dwelling in me, and I mistakenly think I am an independent self with my own responsibilities and responses... and thus, I am consciously under the power of the god of independent-self.

Chapter Twenty-one

How Do I Get this Inner Knowing?

Have you grasped what I'm saying? We must have *inner knowing*. Nothing can be a substitute for that. Remember how I said that faith is only completed faith when it has been replaced by conscious assurance—"substance," as Hebrews 11:1 tells us. We have several times emphasized this, and do it again. Throughout life, faith in its initial form is placed in something external, available to me, and desirable . . . and by inner decision of my mind, heart and will I then say, "I'll do that. I'll go there. I'll make that." On the human level, I then put that inner word of faith into action. I take my car and go there. I use my hands and make that. I take that fruit and eat it. And then what happens? When it reaches out to something, that first inner form of faith is dissolved and replaced by outer facts. It is no longer "I'll go to that home." No! Now I am in that home. Not "I'll eat that." No! It is food in me. Not "I'll make that." No! Here it is, made. The taker's taken! My bodily actions have turned the faith into substance.

But now we are talking about a faith-leap into the *real* dimension—the kingdom of God—the invisible realm of reality with Father, Son and Spirit; and we who are born-again know that when our faith became "substance" we came to a new kind of assurance—ridiculous to the world—in which the Spirit, not human actions, was the agent which brought faith into substance; and that new-birth certainty is nothing but *inner knowing*—a nonrational knowing. *We just know that we know*, and neither man, heaven nor hell can move us. Just as Paul almost shouted to the Galatians, when beginning his letter to them: "I so know this new revelation (of the inner union of Galatians 2:20) in my inner being that if an angel from heaven, or I myself, preach to you any other gospel, let him be accursed!" That, surely, is inner knowing.

And now it is this *second* inner knowing we are talking about, which was so plainly demonstrated by Paul himself in his cry of distress turned into a shout of praise and assurance (Romans 7 and 8). And I am asking, "Do I know that?" Yes, I do. Do you? Don't deceive yourself; don't mistake your first believing of outer given facts for the spontaneous inner knowing. Get it clear. Faith starts off by my attaching myself to something. We have instanced food, a chair, going to a home. But that's not what makes it real to me. It is the response back, like an echo, from the thing to which I am attaching myself which makes the inner knowing. I take the food; I am conscious of it inside me. I sit in a chair; the chair makes me know it is holding me. *That* is the knowing. So the knowing does not come from my putting my faith into something, it comes from the something in which I put my faith. I must never mistake my faith in its first form—my attaching myself to something—for the completion of faith by which it has attached itself to me. Do you see this? So the final knowing of my

How Do I Get this Inner Knowing?

eternal union—that it actually is *He* inwardly joined to me: that it is now *He* living in me, and *not* I—comes from Him the Spirit, and not from me the believer. *He* turns the faith into substance: absolute certainty.

So don't try any imaginings on this level, or try to make yourself *think* you have it. Don't *try* anything, for once again that is this old "self-effort stuff" we have died to. No, I keep doing my part, which is constantly affirming that *what the Scriptures have said about my union with Christ is fact*. I have been and am crucified with Him. I am dead to sin. I am crucified to the world. I now live in His resurrection. No, it is not I, it is He living in me. I *have* said it, and *still* say it. But keep this clear: My saying it is not yet Him saying it back to me. *That* you do not "try" to make up, or feel, or have any scraps of self-effort in it. No, it "comes down from heaven"! How? When? That's not my business. Keep off the grass! Don't inquire. Don't occupy yourself with hoping or waiting. No, remain steadfast in your part of the bargain—affirming the fact on the basis of God's Word even if it is not yet inwardly confirmed to you as fact. And when and how will you know? Neither I nor an angel from heaven could tell you, because it is the prerogative of God Himself, God the Spirit, to speak that inner word. All we humans can say is "You'll know when you know!" Sometimes at once, sometimes after a time-gap.

I did not lightly move into my part of the believing. After five night-hours of battling around with it (so little did I understand the ease of faith in those days), I did finally put my finger on Galatians 2:20, or at least on the first phrase of it, and said right out, "I am crucified with Christ." Then I added a little bit of confessing with my mouth, which Paul said confirms the inner believing: I took a post card, drew a tombstone, and wrote, "Here lies N.P.G., crucified with Christ." I had not reached far out into my resurrection by then!

But did I feel different or know anything different? No. My precious wife, Pauline, was with me and did the same. We had those five hours sitting in our little camp chairs in the forest, in the banana plantation of a precious African brother we had gone to visit. But the Spirit responded more quickly to Pauline. Within two weeks she felt what she took to be a touch on her shoulder, beneath the mosquito net on her camp bed. It was the Spirit confirming her word of faith, and she knew and has known ever since. Next morning, as we sat outside the little native hut we had been staying in, breakfasting at our camp table, she began to say to me that she had something to tell me; but I said, "No need, your face shows it"— and her life has showed it all these years since. But for me, perhaps because I was more a "thinker-through" of a thing, and a slower believer, it wasn't until two years later that the inner light was turned on in my consciousness. During those two years I never went back on that crisis of affirming faith. It had been as serious to me as a wedding ceremony (yes, faith is serious business). So it was background fact to me as I continued my missionary village travelings. But not until I was home on furlough, and speaking with Mrs. Penn-Lewis, a woman of God whose writings had first helped me into this understanding of Romans 6-8 and Galatians 2:20, was this light inwardly turned on in me. I brought some missionary problems to her. But I think she sensed *I* was the problem, because she answered by what she called her "baptism in the Spirit"—not by some outer sign, but by an inner revelation of Him in her, so great that, as she spoke that day to a group of young women, the Holy Spirit brought them all down on their faces to the ground. But the point to me was not her story but that as she spoke, *I knew.* How? I don't know. But I *knew*, and that was a great number of years ago. And *I still know.* Just as certainly and clearly as I knew by the inner witness on the day I came to Christ that I was born again. That's how I know; and you know, or will know in God's time. He confirms what we have affirmed. That's all.

But I do know that as He thus became inwardly real to me, as the One living my life, I did move into an inner knowing which was and is equivalent to saying *It is He living in me and not I.* I was conscious of *Him only* doing the thinking and speaking, *He, not I.* Yet of course it was and is I. And I still have that inner knowing of it being *He, not I.* So it is not difficult for me to say that it is Christ speaking, willing, thinking, acting. It is Christ in His Norman form. It is that Spirit who Jesus said speaks *in* us (Matt. 10:20)—not to us, but *in* us and *by* us: "For it is not ye that speak, but the Spirit of your Father which speaketh in you." It is "God working in us, to will and do of His good pleasure" (Phil. 2:13). So He is the willer and doer, and I just as spontaneously express His willing and doing in my actions.

Chapter Twenty-two

One, Yet Two–a Paradox

But even then, as I've described, when it came to the down-to-earth issue of saying "I am crucified with Christ" with true faith in my heart, there was a five-hour battle. How did I do it? I find that there is *one central obedience* in the Bible. It is mentioned in the last verse but one of the Roman letter—"the obedience of faith." We have been far more used to hearing about works-obedience: "You'll get there by Bible reading, by prayer, by church attendance, by varied activities"; and so we've missed out on this one, central "obedience of faith." But acceed to *it* and all the other obediences will fit in and follow naturally. And this is the easy one. It is simply saying what the Spirit through the Word tells us to accept as *facts* about Christ, *and believing them.*

A battle it was . . . believing and saying that I am what He says I am. Faith is a battle for one basic reason—because we have been so used to believing the common delusion about ourselves: so weak, so wayward, so temptable, yet supposedly I am responsible to improve myself. Therefore this faith-obedience means replacing those old negative-believings by His new positive word. So that I do.

Probably my main believing is first on the *death* side of my identification with Him, because of my negative ideas about myself. That was why I drew a tombstone rather than a picture of resurrection! I had first to see that my old self was really out of its old sin-Satan relationship and dependence, despite human appearances—even though it was joined to Christ more in His death than in His resurrection.

However, the death side of our relationship must not remain in the foreground. The cross is the gateway to "the life," which is the living Christ Himself. "Take my life, and let it be a hidden cross revealing Thee," wrote C.T. Studd. To find and be in a faith-relationship to the death of Christ is a total necessity, but is only the background to "the life." For "the life" is meant to be in the foreground.

My first emphasis has to be on knowing that I really died with Him, because of my years of false condemnation of myself while being apparently alive in the flesh. Even Jesus remained three days in the grave—so it may take us each a little time to realize that "I am in that tomb with Him," so far as my self being enslaved to sin and self-effort is concerned. But it is important to have it clear that when I say "I am crucified with Christ" I do not mean that I as a self have died to being a self—which is an absurdity. Yet preachers often mistakenly use the phrase "death to self." I cannot die to self, for I am eternally a self! I only die in the sense that my self has changed masters. I have "died" to having a job in a steel firm, if I've crossed over and joined a cotton firm. That is the sense in which I have died in Christ.

There are also teachers who put such a strong emphasis on this death reality of the Romans 6 "death to sin" that they leave folks tossing about in a death-mindedness. It is necessary for a time, but then out we come from the tomb!

So Paul continues, in his famous Galatians 2:20 statement, with " . . . nevertheless I live; yet not I, but Christ liveth in me," and we continue in our faith affirmation along with him. We say categorically, and with no ifs or buts, "I am crucified with Christ"—cut off, dead to sin, dead as the old self which was Satan's dwelling place, dead to the world system in which I outwardly live. Dead, dead, dead, in His death. That I have to say before I can move on. But then I say, " . . . nevertheless I live"—meaning, of course, by His resurrection out from the tomb.

But here comes the vital spot. Paul does not stop there one moment in his saying " . . . nevertheless I live." He does not leave us time to dwell on this fact of being risen, alive in Christ. He straightway corrects himself—contradicts himself—and says, "No, not I, but Christ lives in me." Now this is revolutionary, radical, because though he says it is Christ living in me, he is not saying "side by side with me." He is saying Christ has *replaced* me at my center: " . . . *yet not I.*" Or as some have translated it, " . . . yet no longer I." And that is why I use the word *replacement* as a key word.

Now this brings us to the very center of our Total Truth. Paul is obviously really saying, "The real 'I' in me is not my Paul 'I,' but Christ. I am really Christ in His 'Paul' form." Yet *I* am that self-form, for Paul goes on to say in this same scripture, " . . . and the life which I now live in the flesh . . . . " He is still there, the redeemed "Paul-I."

This is the spot where we sometimes meet with controversy. Paul is not here making the point that we are two—Christ and I. No, he is saying right out that the *real* "I" is Christ, and *my* "I" merely His agent, vessel, branch. And he states it so boldly when he puts it, "I live, *no not I,* but Christ lives in me."

Certainly I remain, and (as we shall see later) come right back into the foreground. For Paul speaks of the self in that great Galatians 2:20 statement on *three levels.* I call it moving from *old self* ("I am crucified") to *no self* ("I live; yet not I, but Christ") to *new self* ("the life which I now live in the flesh"); so back we have come to our own selves. But we will look at that new self later. At this crisis moment we center our faith-attention on this middle *no self*—for this is the crux.

We do not find ourselves as the liberated, spontaneous new selves until we have first disappeared to reappear! We have to know ourselves—of course, by the inner knowing of the Spirit—as replaced I's. It is I, yet not I, it is He! It really is He in place of me, and yet here I still am! What a paradox! I turn up again all right, but only on the other side of a fixed, conscious replacement. And it is the coming short of this replacement realization—or indeed, opposition to it—that blocks us right the way through from that total "seeing through" which goes on to seeing *Him only*, not only in the personal, but in the universal.

Chapter Twenty-three

I Know that I Know

We will take the risk of repetition and again go over this crisis moment of truth because of its critical importance—our conscious possessing of our possessions, our second leap of faith. We began our faith-leap by believing in our hearts and confessing with our mouths that we are crucified with Christ. Now we complete it by saying just as definitely the middle section of Paul's Galatians 2:20, "Nevertheless I live; yet not I, but Christ lives in me."

I *say* it. Is that all? Yes, it basically is all; for faith, as we have already said, is thought—thought expressed by word. As a condition of faith, something must be both available and desirable; I'll do no more than think about it until it plainly is both of these. Now to get specific: Nothing could be more desirable to me than that *Christ living in me as me* should be a realized fact. And I've already seen in God's Word that it is available. So it is available and desirable—my mind and heart have those two facts settled. So then what do I do? What I do always when I act by faith. I speak the word, which Paul calls the "word of faith." I say to God, and to myself, that

I Know that I Know

I am now what Paul says he and we are . . . in this great statement of his.

I say it, whether inwardly in my spirit or vocally in words. But then, like Pilate, "What I have said, I have said." That is a solemn verbal affirmation. Probably we do well to say it by confession to another, by making a date in our Bible, or whatever. It is like the purpose behind a public wedding: to make the marriage contract legally irrevocable in the sight of all men. So now this is our leap of faith. We have declared as fact what we have read of with our eyes, what has registered in our minds as plain and intelligible, and what we now choose in our heart to affirm—with no proof beyond those outer responses of my eyes, mind, emotions. That is why faith is a leap—into the yet unprovable. Available, desirable, but not yet reliable. But this is the necessary leap I personally must take. It is the one and only basic obedience of the believer—that "obedience of faith": not of works or some outer activities; no, of faith—which simply means inwardly committing myself to something (Someone) whom I now take to be total reality to me.

I have, of course, this big advantage: I already have in my new birth the saving faith which has become inner substance to me by the witness of the Spirit to the Word. So I already know Him. But this now is Total He, in me, as me—He in my form—or whatever phrase we are best accustomed to. The only outer action involved in this obedience of faith is something which verbalizes this belief in my heart—something which can be called confessing with my mouth. This is only because, for humans, contracts are valid only when there has been some public signing.

But let me again and again make this abundantly clear: Faith is *substantial*. Faith is the substance of the things hoped for, the *evidence* of the unseen. Therefore faith does not merely mean I have done *my part* by just believing and outwardly confessing. *That* is merely *my* faith attachment to something I desire to experience. I take food—no, food *takes me*: *then* faith is substance. I sit on a chair, yes, but the chair *upholds me*, not I it! Faith is *substance*: it produces *certainty*. "I *know* whom I have believed," says Paul. I believe first and *then* know, and in my new birth that inner knowing of the Spirit-reality became so much everything to me that outer things are no longer the real substance I mistakenly thought they were. Now *inner knowing, Spirit knowing,* has become the substance that not world nor flesh nor devil can take from me.

So now in this *second* crisis of faith. Faith is substance. That substance does not come from us who do the believing and committing, but comes from that to which we have committed ourselves. The substance is the food, not the faith that takes it. The substance is the chair, not my faith that commits myself to it. And now the substance, the certainty, is that by some means, at some time—often immediately but not always—the witnessing Spirit *inwardly confirms to me* that it is He, no longer I, living my life. *I know.* I knew fifty-one years ago, fourteen years after my first knowing of salvation, and, of course, I know the same reality today. It is as natural to me as my initial experience of salvation, only greatly enlarged and established as years have gone by. The "believings" of the first part of the last chapter in John's First Epistle have dissolved into "knowings" by the last half, and the key word comes in the middle (1 John 5:10): "He that believeth on the Son of God hath the witness in himself." Then John continues: "These things have I written to you that believe . . . *that ye may know that ye have eternal life* . . . . We *know* that whosoever is born of God sinneth not . . . and we *know* that we are of God . . . and we *know* that the Son of God is come, and hath given us an understanding, that we may *know* Him that is true; and we are in Him that is true" (vss. 13, 18, 19, 20).

So you see, we don't "work up" the knowing. Should you be reading this and say, "Well, I've said that 'word of faith'; I *have believed*, but I can't say *I know*," then don't, don't try to know. Knowing does not come from self-effort; that would be back under the law of "you ought" again. The knowing comes from the Spirit. So what you do is to keep firmly affirming that *you are* what you have now said you are by faith. Your job is to maintain the affirmation. The confirmation comes from Him, and any trying or searching of your own will only insert a fog of unbelief which hinders the Spirit from giving the confirmation. But there *is* the confirmation.

What more perfect pattern are we given of what a normal person is than Jesus Himself? He continually called Himself the "Son of man" (His favorite and most used name for Himself) because He was affirming in no uncertain terms that He was one of us, as us—indeed, was the sole representative of the human family. As Paul said, He came, "made of a woman and made under the law"; and Peter calls Him our "example." And nothing about this ideal man (and we owe it to John that he so clearly observed and presented Him to us in His true self) is more striking than His constant disclaimer of doing anything or being anything *of Himself*. "I do nothing of Myself," John quoted Him several times as saying. When questioned about His work, He said, "The Son can do nothing of Himself, but what He seeth the Father do"; and about His statements, "As I hear, I judge"; and finally, when asked by Philip to show them the Father, to whom He said He was soon going, He gave them this startling answer: "He that hath seen Me hath seen the Father."

This was at the last supper, when it was His definite intention of explaining to them what His own inner (not outer) relationship was to the Father, whom they had regarded as "up" in heaven. He knew He was now leaving them in His physical, outer presence, to return to them as the Spirit in them; so He opened to them how He as *pattern man* had lived His life on earth. "If you've seen Me, you've seen the Father." Then He made the relationship still more marvelously clear by adding, "The words that I speak unto you I speak not of Myself; but the Father that dwelleth in Me, He doeth the works."

So that is what a "normal" man is: not himself, but God dwelling and working in him. Ours is not a God afar off, but God within. In light of this Jesus said, "I and My Father are one"; yet within that union They were two—"I and My Father." And the whole point is that this is not a description of Himself as Jesus the Son of God, unique and different from us, but of Jesus as the Son of man, of whom it says in the Epistle to the Hebrews that "He that sanctifieth and they that are sanctified are all of one, for which cause He is not ashamed to call them brethren."

Jesus Himself had prayed that we should all know this same oneness with each other: "I in them, and Thou in Me, that they may be made perfect in one." And John wrote in his letter that categorical statement, "As He is, so are we in this world"; and "If we love one another, God dwelleth in us, and His love is perfected in us"; and "He that dwelleth in love dwelleth in God, and God in him."

We do remain ourselves—very much ourselves, as we shall be seeing—just as Jesus was so much Himself that the world could never ignore Him as the perfect man, whether they believed in His deity or not. Yet it is *this* upon which we are centering our attention: There was never a moment when He did not know that He and His Father were in an eternal *union*, so that who He was, was the Father being manifested in and through His Son. So our being rebuilt as whole persons must first have *our union* with God through His Son established, and only then do we also freely live in the easy paradox of also being ourselves.

Chapter Twenty-four

Union Reality and the Charismatic

A question that will arise in many minds is whether what millions today speak of as "the baptism in the Spirit" is the same experience as this second crisis of faith of which we are speaking. By "baptism in the Spirit" I mean the most amazing phenomenon of living Christianity today—an experience of the Spirit, usually accompanied by speaking in tongues, commonly called "pentecostal" and nowadays "charismatic." It *is* amazing, because what was once regarded as some weird manifestation confined to a far-out group of people called Pentecostals, who were often given a contemptuous title such as "holy rollers," has now burst through into all the denominations of the church, both Roman Catholic and Protestant, with such dramatic effects that they are welcomed as new quickenings of the Spirit by some ... and opposed as dangerous or even demonic extravagances by others. But it is certainly widespread enough today for this question to be asked.

The first Pentecost, forty days after Christ's ascension—an event He had told His disciples to await as "the promise of the Father" and taking the form of their "receiving power after the Holy Ghost has come upon you"—came with electric effect on those waiting 120. Outwardly it was a rushing mighty wind and cloven tongues as of fire, and inwardly an upsurge of the Spirit which caused them to speak in other languages. Although not in such a dramatic form as that first Pentecost, many thousands of Christians today bear witness to a like experience—usually accompanied by the speaking in other tongues and resulting in a radical change of life and a new enthusiasm for Christ by its recipients. But while this was the great transforming event of the early church and by it the Holy Spirit was experienced in His power, it did not by itself establish in them this total inner knowing of the risen Christ as their permanent Indweller, as the One who so replaced them that they could say with Paul, "I live; yet not I, but Christ liveth in me."

Paul himself was filled with the Holy Ghost at his conversion, when Ananias laid hands on him; but it was only later, after three years alone in Arabia, that he had that "Christ in you" revelation about which he wrote to the Galatians in such absolute terms that to preach any other gospel would be anathema.

And still more strikingly is this plain with Peter, whom we might almost call "Mr. Pentecost," for he had been the spokesman for the disciples at Pentecost. Yet years later, when he visited the live, mostly Gentile church in Antioch, what he still lacked surfaced in public form. This church had such freedom from the do's and don't's of the law that Peter, though at first enjoying it with them, panicked and drew back from this new-found liberty. A group of Jewish Christians claiming to represent James, the head of the mother church in Jerusalem, had come, saying that such liberty was license, and calling on those who were circumcised to make a stand in opposing it. Peter was so frightened by this delegation that he, with others, even including Barnabas, cut himself off from such free fellowship as eating with the Gentiles.

And what did that expose in Peter? Paul told him of his hypocrisy, and it was serious enough to necessitate making a public stand against Peter. What a crisis, a historic moment in the infant church! So Paul "withstood him to the face," and what he told Peter was his revelation in Arabia which included this famous Galatians 2:20 reality—that the Holy Spirit was not only a power as experienced in the baptism of Pentecost, but the actual indwelling Christ Himself replacing Peter in his inner center.

And the evidence that Peter did not yet know this Total Truth was plain for all to see. If Peter had known not only the power of the Spirit but *the living Christ within, replacing himself,* when these Judaizers came to rebuke the "lawless liberty" within the Antioch church, Peter would have recognized his human fear as just an external temptation, such as we all have. He would have known how to replace that outer invasion of fear by the reality of Christ within him confirming the new freedom. But God used this negative situation to bring out this glorious "identification truth" for all the centuries. For it was then that Paul spoke the great Galatians 2:20 inspired word, and in effect said to Peter, "Peter, you don't yet know this. I didn't either, until years after my baptism in the Spirit it was revealed to me in Arabia. You, Peter, are crucified with Christ . . . and instead of being your old, fearing self, you now have *Christ Himself* in you. He has replaced your human fears by confirming in you the liberation He has brought to us all from those old Jewish legalisms. If you had known this you would have stood firm with us all, even against the Jewish leaders. Learn that, Peter."

From all this we learn a lesson of fundamental importance. It is a glorious experience when God confirms His presence in us by His gifts of the Spirit, as He did at Pentecost. This is a gracious manifestation of the Spirit as power, and produces such marvelous effects on us that at first we may think we now have all. But in fact, that first impartation of power has to be inwardly expanded . . . through our personal pilgrimage in the delusion of self-effort living in Romans 7, and then through the wide-open gateway into the full freedom of Romans 8. *Then* He is known and established in us as the living Person He is, not merely manifested in power. By Him living His own total overcoming life in us, we are adequate for every situation.

Therefore those who have experienced the baptism of the Holy Spirit—with the sign or gift of tongues, or other gifts—have been highly privileged in this great steppingstone into Christ as all in all. We can then expand that great primary experience into its full reality by moving in by faith into the "Christ is all and in all" of Colossians 3:11. Today I often find that those who have had a charismatic experience more readily respond to the revelation of the total Christ-union-and-replacement reality than do those who are inclined more to the objective relationship with Christ, as apart from us in His risen and ascended position at the right hand of God. Though they know and love the Lord, they're often fearful of and cautious about too close an approach to Paul's mystery, "hidden, but now made manifest to His saints, . . . which is Christ in you, the hope of glory." Some even label it as some form of "mysticism," dangerous and fanatical.

For myself, as I have many world-wide contacts with God's people of all nations, I cannot conceive how any of my evangelical brethren really oppose as of the flesh or devil all these mighty world-wide manifestations of the Spirit, call them Pentecostal or charismatic. I cannot see how any honest person can attribute the experience of all these we meet with, these who so fervently love and worship Jesus in charismatic assemblies, to being erroneous and warn against them. To me it comes close to blasphemy against the Holy Spirit.

For myself, I esteem my Pentecostal brethren as better than myself and rejoice in fellowship with them as part of them, as I also do with all who preach Christ, whatever lesser differences of interpretation we may have. So when any of these brethren take a position that "you ought to have what we have," I say, "You may be right; pray for me. But I can receive and experience only what the Holy Spirit Himself confirms to me and works in me."

But divide from any? No. We are already one in Christ and we bless each other in the name of the Lord. Wisdom is justified of *all* her children.

Chapter Twenty-five

I Get Myself Back

Now we move on to the surprising and glorious effects on us of this total relationship of replacement-union. The chief one is the paradox.

A person might think that this inner consciousness of Christ in me, as me, would give me an enlarged consciousness of Him and an increased glorying in Him. It does... even though He has already been, for years, my precious Christ in the love relationship of the Song of Songs. But what becomes paradoxically new to me is a totally new *self-acceptance*. And here, at once, we move onto "dangerous ground"—not dangerous to us, but to onlookers like the daughters of Jerusalem in the Song! Because it seems to produce a newly inflated ego—I! It does. But of course, we who have entered in and are now in on the secret know the *whole* key—that it is a Satan-expressing ego which has first disappeared forever in His cross, before reappearing as our new Christ-expressing ego. But it is a total *re*appearing of the "I"! Why? Because it has been God's fixed plan of grace from before the foundation of the world that He was going to have a vast company of fully liberated sons—liberated fully to be themselves—by whom He would fully be *Himself* embodied in human forms. Yet in that paradoxical relationship, unintelligible to those not initiated into it, the human "I" is its full spontaneous self, and acting as such. That is why I often say there is no egoist in history equal to our Lord Jesus Christ! He was always *I, I, I*—"*I* am the door," "*I* am the living bread," "*I* am the light, "*I* am the way." *Emphatic self.* Yet we who know Him are also aware—look within Him!—that He was always saying "I do nothing by Myself, but only what I see My Father do," and "If you see Me, you see the Father."

That is precisely what happens to us. Before we know our exchanged life, while still in the struggles and self-condemnation of Romans 7, we dislike and downgrade ourselves—"O wretched man that I am!" We are compulsively negative about ourselves and deeply suspicious of what we think are our dangerous tendencies. So now it is an altogether new thing, and may take a little time to sink into us, that so far from downgrading ourselves, *because He now accepts us, we now accept ourselves* as His precious vessel, branch, body member, bride. Every part of us—our physical appetites, our soulish emotions and reasoning powers—are beautiful and wholly valuable as His outer means of manifestation. It usually takes a little time to realize this, just because we've been so used to thinking the opposite about ourselves.

So now we're free to be ourselves, because we now know *we are wholly His human forms.* We live with raised, not lowered heads! Sure, we're not unaware of the subtle misuse today by psychologists and many others of a false "self-acceptance" and "self-liberation to be ourselves." Indeed, this is universal, because the deceived natural man assumes he has no self *except* himself, and his only remedy for his self problems is the fraudulent build-up of himself as "inherently good." But just because there is a wave of modern, false emphasis on the build-up of self, that must not inhibit us from boldly accepting and affirming ourselves—we who truly know who we truly are!

One notable effect of this is also another kind of paradox—in that in our normal daily living, for most of the time, we forget who we are, and just function as ourselves. It is the same principle as in our professional lives. Once we are competent in our particular profession, as we've said before, whether a cook, teacher, carpenter, engineer, or whatever, we do not spend our hours reminding ourselves or others that we are this or that, but we just go ahead being it. We don't keep saying "I'm a teacher, I'm a teacher," but we just teach! So in precisely the same way, when we know that we are really He in us, we don't keep running around reminding ourselves or telling that to others. We just do our daily job, enter into our daily conversations, etc., totally forgetting that it is He in us by us—but it *is* only He, all the time. So we don't have to have special prayer times to "remind ourselves," though we love any chances we have for our secret inner-love tryst with Him. Nor do we have to come to the end of a busy day and condemn ourselves for not having thought more of Him. If we do that, He tells us not to be so foolish . . . for our doings and talkings were His all the time.

I don't think my friend, Gloria, sister of former-President Carter, will mind me telling this story about her. About eight or more years ago we were together at a Faith at Work conference in Georgia, and during the weekend the Lord revealed to her the secret that she was really Christ in her form. When she returned home to Plains, she found a card in the mail asking her to speak on herbs at her garden club. But she told me that she knew little about herbs, so she spent the next day or two studying up on them. Then, after having given her lecture and returned home, she talked to the Lord in her room and asked His forgiveness because she had forgotten about Him those days because of her herb preparations. The answer He gave her: "What are you apologizing to Me for? I was co-herbing with you. That was My lecture, not yours!"

So we actually *are* free persons and learn to recognize ourselves as such—free to express our opinions, to make our judgments, to do our jobs, make our choices. Dangerous? It surely looks like that, and others would tell us it is—who don't know the spontaneity of the union. But no danger to us who know our *unchangeable oneness*. We know that all we do is *He,* and we live the "dangerous life" of believing . . . which is knowing and thus recognizing that it is all He. We live spontaneously. If we cook, it is He doing the cooking. If we do our job, it is He doing it. If we have conversation, it is He conversing. Union in the Spirit is actual, factual. Where He is, we are. Where we are, He is. No hairbreadth separation between us can ever be possible.

Chapter Twenty-six

Yes, I Am

I have to say again and again that this union life is different from a committed, dedicated relationship to Christ in which we still see ourselves as two and thus are occupied in depending on Him and receiving from Him the immediate supplies for life. *Union* is different. It is radical because I have stepped right over the line into "Him as me" as well as acknowledging "Him in me." Yes, He *is* in me; I am I and He is He. We are two—yet that's not what I live by. It is *union*—and in the union He is so much my all, and I nothing, that I live with Him *as* me! I talk the language of *Him* being the one thinking, choosing, acting—when it is really I. Enormous, glorious paradox! I thus speak of "replacement."

Less than that is still short of a union leap. I may be saying "I have all—I in Him and He in me," but I'm having to keep closing a gap. Here am I, here is He—and He's doing these things for me: providing power, grace, victory, faith . . . and I receiving them. But this is *not* the same as you or I experiencing them all *as* me. No gap there!

This is why I gave this book the title of YES, I AM. It sounds bold and boastful, and is meant to be, because this is the missing truth about ourselves which is restored only in this union reality. We had, as selves, to go through the process of deceived self, then through self dead to sin and Satan, and thus pass out of self-condemnation into where the central fact now is, He is fully formed in us (Gal. 4:19). But thereby we discover *right self*. The whole purpose of God is that we should be the total persons by whom He can express His total self. So back we come again. Probably when we first experience our union reality it is *He* whom we are seeing and rejoicing about—He in us, as us. But then the further light dawns. *We* are real persons and are meant to be, just as a head can be in action only through its body. *We* rise and shine for our light has come. And how can we now accept and love ourselves as Jesus told us we must? Because we now know that He loves and accepts us to the total degree that He has made us His permanent abode. "The life I now live in the flesh," Paul confidently said, "I live by the faith-recognition that He has loved me and given Himself for me." So I then surely can love myself. If I'm good enough for *Him*, then I'm good enough for myself. This is something really new and fresh when it comes to us. At least it was to me. I am to drop those belittling, downgrading statements about myself. If I am an earthen vessel, it doesn't mean earthy in a derogatory sense, but "human"; and He was human, and God was manifested in that humanity.

So I am no longer a wretched man, but a whole (and holy) man. I am to be myself! Unafraid. *Yes, I am,* and like Paul, I can do all things in Christ, as Christ. I am well able (like Caleb). I'm full of power and of judgment and of might (like Micah). I am my

Beloved's and His desire is toward me (as His spouse) (S. of S. 7:10).

Once the Savior knew at His baptism that the moment of His commissioning had come as the Christ of God, He never once hesitated in saying, "I am...", "I am...", "I am..."; and they crucified Him for it. And I must not hesitate to be *my* "I am." If I am now an equipped, anointed, indwelt son of God, I say so. Yes, *I am.*

Chapter Twenty-seven

A Woman and a Man Tell It

Here are two letters which show the same thing. They show the difference which realizing who we are makes in our thinking and acting. They make it plain that even committed, consecrated servants of Christ may be living with a conscious inner gap between themselves and Him. When the storm blows, that Christian finds himself at one end of the boat sinking, while Christ is asleep at the other—and he has to call on Him to awake and save him! What a difference when the Christian realizes that there is no difference—that Christ is on the boat in him, as him—and when the sea gets rough, he rebukes the storm as He.

The first letter comes from a friend of many years, Cally Gordon, now a widow with her five children in their early twenties and upward. She has been involved in the Lord's work for many years, and we've had many meetings and conversations together. She was with us in our Wisconsin Conference, and then in the home of Dr. John and Linda Bunting, in Louisville, Kentucky, which is really a family home to us in our Union Life fellowship, and where a number of us gather for our annual family fellowship. She writes:

> To say the least, my time with you all meant a transformation in my thoughts. Suddenly everything I had read, heard and talked with you about in the past twenty years seemed to "jell" and become a reality. It became *me*! It was almost like a miracle! And ever since, I've experienced something within—which for so many years was more intermittent, but which now has become continuous, and which also has become a definite part of my consciousness—or really, which has become me. It's like a long voyage (learning is), and finally arriving at my destination. So in actuality (slowly arriving after all these years) the new "me" is really Christ as me. I know it, I live it, and it's a reality not just occasionally or after "down times," but all the time.
>
> During these twenty-odd years, by talks, letters, et cetera, something real was actually transpiring in a tangible way, a new or increased consciousness was becoming me. But going to the Union Life Conference Center in Wisconsin (before going on to the Louisville conference) was God's way for me to finally emerge from my cocoon and into the miracle of knowing who He is and who I am (that knowing within the deepest part of me); and the fetters of concern or worry of what is happening and why—the hurts of life, etc., which come to all of us—all began to fall off. I know the hurts will come, but I know what to do with them. (I knew before, but somehow there was a block somewhere in me which allowed them to remain in me, even though as a shadow.)
>
> So now I live in the center of me. I live from the

real me, and not in the appearance of things which come and go. I cannot convey to you (or can I?) the true sheer joy of arriving home, finding in truth and in reality Him as me. In the past, the knowledge in my head was frequently forgotten for a time, with the illusion that all the painful experiences were the reality. Even though I'd try not to believe this, nevertheless the pains of the hurts caused me, for a moment, to forget that knowledge. I had learned about Reality v. illusion. Apparently God has a time for all of us to *know*, to reach that destination within our being where it's not only settled, but there is nothing else but Him to us. Everything now is God. (Of course it always was, but I concentrated on appearances too much.) Circumstances, events, people, actions, everything is He, and my spirit is quiet and one with Him, and that is fixed, not only in my saying it, but because I honestly *know* it.

What a glorious life it really is, to finally arrive home in Him—that's where I live now, and it *works*! So many years of struggle and pain, but that was God's way for me and it was good. I now live in that center. The wind, rain and storms may come and probably will—but I'm not the old me who will be blown about with the pain of them, because I'm fixed forever.

I just had to ramble on, as I knew that you would want to know that these days clinched it all for me. God's time—for me—for that miracle of all miracles, the Knowledge, the Knowing, the Reality (Is there any way to aptly describe it?), the glorious Constant Consciousness of that mystery "Jesus as me." What a relief. I've come to Rest!

The second letter is from a stockbroker, Robert Chamberlain. He writes:

On February 20, 1973, at the age of 21, I asked Jesus to forgive my sins and come into my heart. Twelve days later, in a charismatic church, I indicated my desire to be filled with the Holy Spirit. So I was taken to the prayer room along with a few others and we all received instructions about how to "receive." Shortly after several people had laid their hands on me and began praying, I experienced what charismatics frequently label as "the baptism with signs accompanying."

Two years later, in January 1975, I was involved in the biggest decision of my life. At this point I recognized that up to that time in my life I had not experienced what Norman Grubb refers to as the "second crisis." But I was unfamiliar with his books at that time. I merely knew before that I *did not* do God's will, but now I realized that I *could not* do God's will. What a predicament! I prayed. I read. I searched for an answer.

During this time I read about such men of God as Charles Finney, Dwight Moody, Hudson Taylor, John Hyde, Rees Howells, and many more. I noticed that most of them spoke of an experience with God, apart from salvation, that drastically changed their lives. After they were saved—after they had done works for God such as starting missions, churches, schools, etc.—after all these things—something happened. They met God in a new way. They called it by various names, but they seemed to share a common experience. This is what I needed. This is what I sought—a deeper experience with God which would radically transform my life to be able to perform that impossible task which was set before me.

In my searching, I came across Norman Grubb's book *The Spontaneous You*, and was greatly blessed. I discovered that Norman had a more recent book entitled *Who Am I?*, so I bought a copy and read it and underlined it, and read it again and again. I knew that this man had what I wanted, and he was trying to share it with me. I prayed the prayer that he recommended about acknowledging "Christ in me," but nothing happened. Still I persisted. I read more of his books and the books of others, mostly biographies of men of God. My hunger increased, and my yearning grew more intense. When would God answer my cry?

I began to have serious doubts about God and about myself. I came dangerously close to turning my back on God, my wife, everything. If God was real, why wouldn't He answer my cry? If He wasn't real, I wasn't going to waste my life "playing church." I was really getting desperate.

On the evening of November 8, 1978, a Wednesday, I was troubled, as usual. I went into my study and shut the door behind me. I talked to God. I don't remember what I said. I flipped through a few books I had on my shelf about men of God. I read Dwight Moody's account of his "baptism in the Holy Spirit" again. I read Hudson Taylor's account of his experience with God after he had been a missionary for many years. I read the book of Romans. In the fourth chapter of Romans I came across the story of Abraham. The following excerpts seemed to come alive to me.

As Paul wrote in Romans 4:3-13 *(NIV)*: "Abraham

believed God, and it was credited to him as righteousness.... To the man who ... trusts God, ... his faith is credited as righteousness.... Under what circumstances was it credited? Was it after he was circumcised, or before? It was not after, but before! And he received the sign of circumcision, a seal of the righteousness that he had by faith while he was still uncircumcised." Then Paul continued: "It was not through law that Abraham and his offspring received the promise that he would be heir of the world, but through the righteousness that comes by faith."

God had given Abraham a promise, I saw. By all human means, it would be impossible for Abraham to ever obtain that promise. Yet, Abraham believed. He didn't understand. He just believed. And because he believed what God had said—even though the thing was impossible—he was righteous. He walked in the truth that God had declared. He assumed the role of the "Father of many nations" even though it was impossible for him and his wife to have a son.

Because Abraham believed God and walked in the truth, he was righteous. Did he feel righteous? Had he any outward signs of being righteous? I think not. He received circumcision much later. The inward reality existed long before the outward evidence appeared. But he was righteous as soon as he believed.

God was telling me to *believe*. The task was impossible for me to perform. But I didn't have to perform it. I had now come to the point where I could appropriate Galatians 2:20: "It's Christ that lives in me." God was going to perform this impossible task in me and through me. I didn't have to do it. God would do it. In fact, it was *already done.* Right from the beginning, I had always been what "I" couldn't become. The truth of Galatians 2:20 became real to me. I now saw what Norman and the others came to see. I read on in Romans 4:18-23: "Against all hope, Abraham in hope believed and so became the father of many nations.... He did not waver through unbelief, ... but was strengthened in his faith and gave glory to God, being fully persuaded that God had power to do what He had promised. This is why 'it was credited to him as righteousness.' The words 'it was credited to him' were written not for him alone, but also for us, to whom God will credit righteousness—for us who believe in Him who raised Jesus our Lord from the dead."

Now, for the very first time, I could see what it was all about. I called to my wife and shared these things with her. I told her that this was what Norman Grubb had been talking about when he spoke of a second crisis. We reread a portion of *Who Am I?*—and Norman said that when you come to this point, you say a prayer acknowledging that it is Christ now living in you; not yourself any longer. I asked my wife, "What shall we do?" There was a long silence. I answered my own question, "I think we have to."

She replied, "We really don't have any choice."

As we realized that Jesus wanted to take over our lives it seemed exciting, except for one fact: in order for Him to live in us, we had to die. That wasn't so exciting. But we prayed the prayer, one at a time in our own words. I really believed. Before I prayed the prayer I expected that at some time—several years later maybe—I would receive a sign or seal of what God had done. But, immediately upon acknowledging that Christ was in me now, something happened. I received a seal upon my heart. No lightning. No choirs of angels. Nothing had changed. And yet, everything was different. It wasn't just a profession by faith. Christ in me was me—is me! He was there all the time—I just hadn't let Him "be" before. At this point I have a hard time trying to explain just what happened. But it happened to my wife, too. Everything is different now for both of us. There is a world of difference between life as we live it now and life as we lived it before.

I had many questions in my mind before this. Questions such as "Who am I? What am I? Who is God? What is life?" and many, many more. Before, these questions haunted me. Now it didn't matter. What matters now is *Christ in me*. Everything else is O.K. The problems are still there—maybe more than before. But now it is O.K. Christ is still there too; and He'll take care of them.

Chapter Twenty-eight

What about Temptation?

This still leaves a major question to be answered. Indeed, it is the chief objection usually raised to such a life as we have now been affirming as ours. *It seems,* they say, *too easy.* Life is not a bed of roses. Life is not lived on a Cloud Nine. What about those areas of our daily living which appear to contradict a life which we say is *not we living it, but He as us*? What about what are certainly temptations, and appear often to be failures and even sins?

Paul and James speak of these aspects of life as temptations and trials (one word covers both concepts in the original Greek). Temptations are enticements to want what we should not; trials are those times when we are faced with what we don't want, but can't avoid!

First then, temptations, which until we have them in right focus are the most troublesome to us. (We'll look at trials in a later chapter.) They are the reason why many people say, "This Christ-in-you life is not livable or workable, because of the way we succumb to so many temptations." Yet we know that temptations are just as continuous in a *perfect* human life, because it is said of Jesus that He "was in all points tempted like as we are, yet without sin" (Heb. 4:15). Therefore temptations and their enticement are part of a perfect, not imperfect life—and are not themselves sin.

So we squarely face constant temptation on this new level of living, just as much as in the former. The question, then, is often asked, "What is it in us which is tempted and responds to temptation, if we are this new man in Christ and say we are dead to sin and have crucified the flesh with its affections and lusts?" The answer is simply that, as we have already said, we are *human selves*, and our oneness with Christ does not alter our two-ness in being He and I. God's whole purpose is to express Himself through our fully human selves, just as He did with Jesus.

So this human self of ours is just as continually tempted as His was. James explains temptation as being related to the obvious fact that I, as a human, have all the human appetites and faculties of soul and body. In fact, it is by these that God manifests Himself through our selves. Our humanity is responsive to what we might call the "upward temptations" of producing the fruits of the Spirit (see how God "tempted" Abraham to sacrifice his son—Gen. 22:1). So also it is fully open and responsive to all the downward temptations of the flesh, world and devil. This world contains every form of solicitation to the lusts of the flesh, the lusts of the eyes and the pride of life, for "the whole world lieth in the wicked one." To these we in our humanity have responded and lived in all our unsaved days. We have been at home in them. So no wonder that we are constantly assailed by such "drawings." For James says temptation is when we are "drawn away by our own desires and enticed" (1:14); and enticement makes us really want to do it. So temptation definitely makes us want to do what we should not.

Now the vital point is to recognize that this is not sin. Scripture clearly states that Jesus was tempted at all points (and that covers a great deal) as we are, so temptation is not sin for He was "without sin." That means He was enticed to do such things and yet never sinned. Therefore, temptation is not sin. We know He was so tempted because we are given one instance when He did temporarily respond to temptation. That was after He had constantly told His disciples that His Father's will was for Him to die and rise again. Yet when the time came, He plainly said He didn't want to die. He was "enticed" to want to escape death and live. "Father, if it be possible, let this cup pass from Me." That was temptation, and He plainly had it. Of course His victory was, "Nevertheless not as I will, but as Thou wilt," and that took three hours of bloody sweat to have it settled.

This is of great value to us. Just because we are so often tempted, just because we feel the various pulls of soul and body, we should not drag our feet under a sense of guilt and false condemnation.

Sin is only when we go a definite further step. When, as James says, "lust has conceived, it brings forth sin." Conception and birth are the results of a marriage union. In other words, we have gone beyond the "wanting" condition to a deliberate, conscious choice of doing the thing; and we don't often go that far.

But now in our union life, a total reversal has taken place: not just a change of our spirit joined to His Spirit, but of the control of our whole personhood, including our soul emotions and body appetites. All are now His property. Our bodies are the temples of the Holy Spirit. Our members are "instruments of righteousness unto God." We are slaves of righteousness, whereas we used to be slaves of sin. We are "renewed in the spirit of our minds," and every thought is being "brought into subjection to the obedience of Christ." There is now this upward pull on our souls and bodies—upward temptation to respond to Him. Our bodies are living sacrifices. We delight to do His will.

This is a radical reversal from our fear of flesh responses and our constant guarding against them. Even though Christians, we have become so used to seeing ourselves negatively: Sex is so dangerous and so close around the corner that we are captured by illicit desires . . . also by greed and love of material things . . . and by jealousy and hate and resentment. We have been afraid of our flesh, and by no means free to fearlessly use our body faculties and soul emotions for Christ and others.

We therefore, in our new union relationship, take a further step of faith on the soul-and-body level. We are firm in faith that we are *kept,* and *He* does the keeping. "Kept by the power of God through faith," wrote Peter. "Now unto Him who is able to keep us from falling," wrote Jude. And said John, "Perfect love casts out fear." So why be fearful?

So, in this new way, we have our emotions to use to express our love and joys and interests, and our minds to be stretched in daily launches of faith in the God of the impossible; our bodies too, appetites and all, are free to express our love and care for others, without being fearful of their misuse. That is our new boldness of faith, though those appetites and emotions have formerly had such a negative hold on us. But fear not. Have faith in the Keeper.

This also gives us a radical change of outlook on temptation. It used to be something to be fearful of, avoid, and feel greatly guilty about; now we see temptation as an asset, not a liability! Why and in what sense? Because light must have darkness to shine out of. Temptations are pulls back to walk again in darkness. But if we now know *who we are,* we see all our temptations as what God is meaning us to have, and each exactly suitable to us. We see them all as opportunities to manifest Him through our souls and bodies. Temptation has become opportunity! We understand why James tells us to count all temptations as *joy. Christ is manifested by them.*

Chapter Twenty-nine

James Explains

But how can we say that it is Christ who is manifested when we are tempted? Let us look at what we do when we are tempted, and then at the remedy for it.

What happens during temptation is that the human part of us is being drawn away by some solicitation to function just as our old flesh-self used to; and what this means is that we temporarily forget who we are. We forget we are Christ in our human form, and we are pulled to respond as if apart from Him. Instead of being in our normal daily condition of subconsciously recognizing that we are in our vine-branch union (which is what Jesus meant by "abiding," which in the Greek means "remaining"), we are diverted into believing in some attractive flesh-response of body or soul; and what we are believing in at any time holds us in its grasp.

Now in our former self-striving life, trying to combat temptation and sin in our own strength, we would try to resist it even while we responded to it and, as a result, have an inner sense of condemnation because we were even dallying with it. But usually the more we resisted and condemned ourselves, the more the thing gained its hold on us. So we lived a fighting, struggling, supposedly two-nature life—the one striving against the other.

But now, in our new understanding, we don't deny or fight the temptation. We do not resist or struggle against it. No, we admit and accept it, because we recognize it is not sin but is the normal pull that the outer world, through the flesh, has on us—as it did on Christ—and that God *means us* to have it. But the importance of accepting, acknowledging, and not resisting is that this "draws the teeth" of the temptation. What you resist, resists you. What you fight, fights you. In this sense I apply Jesus' words, "Agree with thine adversary quickly, whiles thou art in the way with him; lest . . . thou be cast into prison." In other words, acknowledge that he is your adversary, and that will take the bite out of him.

So the result of my accepting and agreeing is that it takes the heat out of any resistance by me, and loosens me from the grip of my diverted believing in this enticement . . . and as I free the temptation to *be* a temptation, I equally free myself from being bound to it by my false believing in it. And I am free to do what? To remember and recognize *who I really am*—Christ in me! Recognition is faith in its completed form. So I recognize that He is *peace* when I am tempted to worry. He is *courage* when fear grabs me. He is genuine *love* for a person I am feeling hatred for. Furthermore, He is *other love* who can reverse my temptation to an illicit love, and can cause me to love that one for his or her own benefit and not for my self-gratification. Since He is all these to me *as me*, *I* am the manifestation of peace, love and power. Christ is the light who uses the darkness as something which, by His swallowing it up, manifests *Him* as light in a new form. If I wasn't tempted to hate, I couldn't experience and manifest His love. If I wasn't tempted to fear, I couldn't experience and manifest His courage. If I wasn't tempted to an illicit love, I couldn't experience and manifest His other-love for the benefit of that person through me. My temptations are my assets in continually manifesting Him in new forms.

This is the way in which we totally reverse our outlook on our temptations. We used to be frightened of them because, while still thinking we were independent selves, we were afraid of ourselves and how we could be captured by sin . . . so we would pray the beginner's prayer, "Lead us not into temptation." But now we see temptation as the adventure of faith! For it is this necessary negative on which the positive of Christ is built. That's why I can say with James that I "count it all joy" (a strong, total word—*count*, not feel) when I have my various temptations.

Let us look a little more closely into how James gives us the remedy for the assaults of all kinds of double-mindedness, in his strongly practical letter. Here we will see works not as antagonistic to faith, but as its fulfillment. The basic question will be, How do we add the right kind of works to our faith?

In this epistle it looks as if we believers have a constant struggle. James speaks of us having the problem of two minds (either believing or wavering); having two standards in our brotherhood relationships (one for the rich but another for the poor); using two tongues (for blessing and cursing); holding two friendships (for the world and for God); having two motives in prayer (self-interest and for others). James mentions all these doubles and presents us as having a conflict between them, with the negative usually overwhelming the positive.

This is a two-nature struggle, all right, and it's set forth in a letter to believing brethren! But now look more closely at the beautiful remedy James slips in for those eager enough to search it out and find it—or, shall we say, who are open to its God-given reality. In the first chapter he speaks of God's goodness in "begetting us with the word of truth"—his expression for the new birth (1:18). But then, he continues, we get mixed up with all kinds of disturbing self-reactions, not yet knowing the remedy for the "self" problem. He calls this "all filthiness and superfluity of naughtiness" (1:21). So what is the answer? We experience it when, by faith, the living word of truth has not only begotten us but is also engrafted into us—his way of describing the vine-branch union relationship—and we become inwardly fixed. This fixedness comes as we see ourselves in union with Christ—that we are forms by which He is manifesting Himself. James calls this blessed insight "the perfect law of liberty" (1:25).

Now he gives this subtle illustration. While we are still in the old self-effort illusion and don't yet know Christ in us as us, we are like a man who looks into a mirror and sees himself just as his normal, helpless self—with no hope of any means of changing himself (1:24). So he just goes away and forgets about it. But, James says, when we know the inner union, He in our form, then when we look into the mirror we no longer see our human, failing selves, we see ourselves as who we *now are:* human expressions of that perfect law of liberty, Christ Jesus, who is the

Spirit of other-love. So now we can go out into life with confidence, because we are no longer just ourselves, we are Christ in us as us.

So now we understand the conflict of these doubles not as the contest of two natures, one pitted against the other; rather, we see the temptation as something not within us but something *seeking to draw us away from who we are*. So we "resist" that drawing not by denying or fighting it but *by recognizing Christ in us as us*. Thus He uses the temptation for a new manifestation of Himself by us.

So, James says, life will always consist of endless trials and temptations, because they are the negatives by which He the positive can reveal Himself. Therefore, when we lack wisdom in a situation and ask for it, let us take it for granted that He is in the process of giving it to us. But along come questionings. Will He really show us what to do? Now if we were in the old two-nature conflict, we should be swinging between faith and doubt; but we, knowing we are He in us, dissolve the temptation by saying, "I'm not taking that temptation to doubt. That is an external assault on me. I'm not double—I'm single. And Christ is my wisdom." The stand of faith dissolves the doubt.

The same is true with our new tongues, says James (3:1–18). Our old tongue is a filthy one; our new tongue glorifies God and blesses man. So what then when our tongue slips back into some negative speaking?—if instead of blessing God we curse men, who are made after the similitude of God? Have we then two tongues, and must we always swing from the one to the other? No, says James, for we are like a fountain of water which can't produce "both salt water and fresh" (*NIV*). We know we are a fountain of fresh water. Therefore, the salt was just something which got mixed up with the water as it flowed out of the fountain. The defect cannot be within the fountain itself, nor can it be in us. So we recognize the wrong things we said as a slip into temptation—not affecting the purity of the fountain in our union reality—and remedied by a word of repentance and cleansing. We no longer live in a struggle between two kinds of speaking, good and evil discourse. We speak positively and lovingly from our love source with what James calls "the wisdom that is from above," rather than from beneath.

Then he raises the question of our motives in prayer (4:1–4). Are they sometimes double, and mainly for our own self-interest? Once that was so, and it caused us to question what we were asking for, as if we lived with double motives. But now we don't. Our motives are pure from their pure center, and we go boldly forward in our prayer requests, asking, as Jesus said, "whatsoever we desire." So we have become established in this glorious fixed reality wherein we see ourselves as the expression of the perfect law of liberty, that law which James also calls "the royal law according to the scripture, Thou shalt love thy neighbor as thyself." And we are that!

And we remain unchanged through all the temptations. "I am single, not double." The assaults of doubleness are only attempts to divert me from my basic singleness. That is why temptations are always such an adventure of faith, and the means of perfecting my faith so that I "count them all joy." Finally, James calls on the brethren to move into this faith union in Christ, and out from that apparent double-mindedness. "Cleanse your hands, ye sinners; and purify your hearts, ye double-minded" (4:8).

There is one further question which is always being asked about the temptation issue—a favorite question. "But what about sin? Do we still commit sins?" Why do people always bring that up? Because, until we have found a way out, we are so congenitally sin-minded. We have become so used to our struggles and failures and guilt—and perhaps we also want some excuse for our continuance in sin!

The usual scripture on which people base that question is 1 John 1:8–9, "If we say that we have no sin, we deceive ourselves.... If we confess our sins, He is faithful and just to forgive us our sins...." But our anxious concern about sin is what gives us away, for the whole point of this summit letter of John's on the union is not about sinning, but our *union reality*. We are in the light as He is in the light (for He is the light in us). We walk as He walked (for He is walking in us). We know all truth (for the Spirit is the knower in us). We live the right life, as He does (for the sin spirit in us has been replaced by the Holy Spirit). We love as He loves (because He is love and dwells in us). We believe as He believes (with the world-overcoming faith of the Son of God). *We are as He is* ("for as He is, so are we in this world"—1 John 4:17). It is the total union level. The totally positive level. We are! We know we are! Yes, *I am.*

But because we have our real, temptable humanity, John started his letter with these *sin* statements. He declares that there is sin, and that if we sin there is this immediate remedy in Christ's blood. If it is quick sinning, it is quick cleansing. Indeed, we add sin to sin if we don't immediately replace the sin and guilt-consciousness with a total forgetting of it in Him of whom it is stated that "our sins and iniquities He remembers no more." We go right ahead praising, and indeed use a sin "slip" once again to magnify the grace of God. The loss turned to gain! But then John also adds, "These things I write unto you that ye sin not." That is all that John has to say in his whole five chapters about the possibility of our sinning. It is a detail to him. We are Christ-minded, not sin-minded. We walk so confidently in our new union-relationship that John says, "Whosoever is born of God doth not commit sin . . . he cannot sin, because he is born of God" (3:9). We cannot return to sin as a principle, but if we do slip into a sin there is the immediate remedy. Confess it and forget it; don't rehash it or ask sin questions. Talk Christ union and live it . . . because we can't help it.

Chapter Thirty

That Soul-Spirit Understanding

All of us in Union Life know that a special key is given us for our daily stabilizing by the writer to the Hebrews. He declares that this life has *rest*, not strain as its basis (4:1-11). It is the rest God has had since He rested on the seventh day after completing the creation. It is also that of Israel entering into the land of Canaan. But he goes on to say that the true rest is what we have in Christ, our Joshua. That rest is by no means a folding of the hands, but a fully active life that is a thrill to live because it has adequacy at its center, not inadequacy. Living life *without* what it takes to live it causes strain; living life *with* what it takes to live it produces rest. The resting life he describes this way: "He that is entered into His rest, he also hath ceased from his own works, as God did from His" (4:10). Living by my own works was when *I* was the worker. The rest-life will have even more works, for *He* is the worker. But that type of working is resting. The key to entering into God's rest and continuing in it is by a revelation nowhere else so clearly stated in the Bible. It is in knowing the difference between soul and spirit (4:12).

We already have seen that the human spirit is the

basic self. Soul and body are the means by which we express ourself and live a fully active life. So as long as we confuse what we are in our inner spirit-self with the ways in which we express ourself by our outer soul and body, we are in trouble.

The writer to the Hebrews likens the difference between soul and spirit to the joints and marrow in our physical bodies. The marrow is what contains the inner life of the bones—a picture of spirit. The joints are the way by which that inner life goes into action in hands and feet, etc.—analogous to soul. And he says we have spirit and soul so mixed up that it takes a revelation for us to see the difference. "For the word of God is quick, and powerful, and sharper than any two-edged sword, piercing even to the dividing asunder of soul and spirit" (4:12).

In simple terms, in our spirits we love. By our soul emotions and body action we express our love. In the spirit we know. By the soul we express our knowledge by our reasoning faculty. (Peter shows the relationship between those two when he says we should be ready to give "a reason for the hope that is in us.") So soul and body are the precious and only means by which we—our spirit, and God's Spirit by us—can express ourselves.

The quality of Spirit-spirit union is stillness, for the universal is always still. "Be still and know that I am God." God spoke to Elijah in a "still, small voice." Spirit can be compared to the sea, which, with its mighty currents and streams, is a "still" source of power; the soul is like the rampaging waves which dash about as the expression of that power. The power is in the sea, and not in the waves.

So our danger and problem—till we are awakened

to it—is in mistaking the surges of the waves (soul emotions) for the unmoved and calm center (spirit). We get into trouble when we mistake the variable emotions of the soul for our still spirit-center. The waves are feelings such as anger, hurts, jealousies, fears, lusts; or alternatively, soul feelings of depression, deadness, uselessness, meaninglessness, coldness, emptiness, inability to believe—an endless list. The same is true of our soul in its reasoning activities: All kinds of disturbing or evil thoughts can pour into us, with all the doubts and questionings they bring, and influence our mental attitudes. Notice that this verse of Scripture also compares soul and spirit to "the thoughts and intents of the heart": intents, our spirit—fixed purpose; thoughts, our soul—varied opinions about the intents.

That is also why John in his First Epistle (3:19-21) makes a differentiation between our hearts and God. He says, "If our heart condemn us, God is greater than our heart, and knoweth all things." "Heart," representing feelings, is soul—and we can get plenty of condemnation in our feelings. But God, who knows all and doesn't condemn, speaks His assuring word into our spirits.

Even so, it is easy, outwardly, to be strongly drawn by some desire of the heart and seem to be helpless against it. But in my spirit-center, where God is, I know my real desire is His will, and He keeps His firm hold on me. A friend recently wrote regarding a strong desire for a certain thing: " . . . but in this I felt myself kept. This keeping made me angry at times, because I wanted to have my own way and I knew I could not. I knew it could never be because that wasn't what the *real me* wanted." Outward and inward desire: the workings of soul and spirit.

A person inquires of me, "What do I do when I say I am 'Christ as me' and yet there is someone I hate?" I laugh and reply, "You are kidding yourself. You don't hate; you can't hate. You can only feel you do on your soul/emotional level and mistake that for hate. Hate is only love reversed—and you are love, which is He in you, and you love by the set purpose of the will; and you know that if the real need arose you would give yourself for the one you 'hate.' While soul love is emotion, spirit love is will—and we are fixed in that kind of love. So we may feel more like hell and yet be in heaven.

So we see ourselves in our spirit-center, where we and He are one in spirit, and all things are ours in Him. Soul and body are our wonderful means of endless spirit expression. And having grasped, by the revelation of the Word, the distinction between soul and spirit, I do not fear my soul and body . . . and still less do I foolishly wish I were without their disturbing reactions. No, I thankfully see myself as a whole person, *God's whole person.* He has equipped me with these fascinating means for living out my full life as a whole self with Himself, in all my life's activities. Because they are wholly His, I will put no limits on the liberated use of my soul and body. At the same time, I totally enjoy the fact that He has me safely in hand, even with the surges of the negatives temporarily flooding in. Spirit wins its battles over soul and body diversions, being "kept by the power of God"; and we, "having all sufficiency in all things, abound unto every good work."

Chapter Thirty-one

On, Now, to the Third Level

We have seen with unmistakable clarity that there are stages in our becoming settled about who we are by grace, and stages through which we must pass; or we can call them grades from which we must be graduated. We have already looked into two of these . . . (whatever name we decide to call them): justification and unification—Christ for us and Christ in us.

But the Bible makes it plain that there are *three* grades, not two—and each equally necessary. We have spent much time on the first two, but it is less recognized that there is a third to be consciously entered into.

In calling them "grades" or "levels of being" there is always a danger that we may slip back into the old snare of self-effort and self-development and think of them as something *we* have to attain to. "Growth," also, is a common concept we use to denote what we think of as spiritual progress. How often I hear it said, "Well, it has taken you time and will take me time to get there." So we need a constant reminder that spiritual growth, or the attaining of a new "grade," is not some form of painfully acquired self-enlargement; rather it is the same old story, nothing but a growth in *recognition* of what Christ, our last Adam, has attained for us . . . which is already ours. That is why growth is spoken by Peter in his Second Epistle with these words: "Grow in grace, and in the knowledge of our Lord and Saviour Jesus Christ." Growth, therefore, is merely the next stage of recognition of who we already are in Him; and that recognition, as we now know, is always and only by the nonworks method of faith, and the Spirit is the one who establishes us.

So with this safeguard, we move on to this third level. The simplest description of the three levels (because he uses a down-to-earth analogy) is John's, when he writes to his readers as "little children," "young men," and "fathers" (1 John 2:12–14). He makes brief comments about what he means, spiritually speaking, by these three stages. A little child is totally dependent externally on his parents and knows nothing but what they outwardly are to him. So a little child in grace knows simply that he was a sinner, that he is forgiven through Christ, and thus, now, God is his heavenly Father. A young man has moved from outer dependence on his parents to finding his own inner resources for life—progress from outer to inner. "I write unto you, young men, because ye have overcome the wicked one . . . because ye are strong, and the word of God abideth in you." This is a plain-spoken description of our being established in the "on top" life which we have spent so long in examining in every detail, and into which we have now moved by the second crisis. We now know we are strong—*and we know why.* Therefore we are no longer tossed about in those old struggles with devil and flesh. We know inwardly, not just outwardly, what first came to us as outer, written word . . . but which now abides in us, fused into our inner consciousness by the Spirit. What a total description of an established, achieved life . . . not of trying, hoping, kind of slipping in and out of it, but *being*!

"I have written unto you, fathers," John states cryptically, "because ye have known Him that is from the beginning." That brings us back to the realization that "knowing" in Scripture usually refers not to mere mental understanding, but implies being mixed with the thing we know. That is why the Bible uses the word for sexual intercourse: "Adam knew Eve his wife." Spiritually, it is inner know-how; and what you know, that you are. "This is eternal life," said Jesus in His great prayer to His Father, "that they might know Thee the only true God, and Jesus Christ, whom Thou hast sent." And we who are born of His Spirit *know* that knowing is the inner union. So when John says that we "fathers" know Him that is from the beginning, he means that, as fathers, we are in inner union with that Eternal One—not in His beginning, but as the One who now, as from the beginning, is in the process of completing what He has begun; and we are involved with Him in that completing process. Amazing grace! The point, then, is that we now are no longer dependent children, but cooperating sons: Father and Sons, Inc.!

What John has given us on its three levels in such understandable terms is seen all through Scripture in those same three forms. We are united with Christ in His crucifixion, resurrection, and ascension—and Paul wrote letters which concentrate on each of these:

Galatians on our identification with Him in His death; Colossians on our being risen with Him; Ephesians on our ascended life, seated with Him in the heavenlies, and its outcome.

Paul's Roman letter we all recognize as his fully developed, detailed, and authoritative statement of what he calls "my gospel." In this letter the three states are plain enough: chapters 3 to 5—justification (little children); 6 to 8—unification (young men); 9 to 15—cooperation, co-saviorhood (fathers).

In Hebrews there are the three again. The writer plainly likens Jesus to Moses because, by the new birth, He saves us out of our Egypt, the world; and to Joshua, because He takes us into the land of milk and honey, the promised rest, after we have emerged from the childhood wilderness. Then he stops short very significantly, and says there is a third likeness: to Melchisedec, king of Salem, priest of the most high God. In this parallel Jesus is our great High Priest. Now whenever there is a *high* priest, there must be other priests serving along with him. But when speaking here of the order of Melchisedec, the writer does not name anyone as co-priests, because those Hebrew believers had a spiritual blockage en route (5:12-6:2), showed negative reactions to their sufferings (10:32-39), and were tied in knots of self-pity (12:5-13). He does, however, describe the co-priesthood of the third level in his famous list in Hebrews chapter 11 of the giants of faith, who were the intercessor priests of their respective generations. And *we* are to be such for our God today, "a royal priesthood" (1 Pet. 2:9).

Chapter Thirty-two

Paul Moving into the Third Level

The most revealing of all analyses of these three grades of experience is by Paul himself in his Philippian letter. In 3:3-14 he pours out to us some of the Lord's dealings with him. He starts by mentioning the many qualifications he had "in the flesh," but plainly states that he no longer has confidence in such things. We can sense his thankfulness for his awareness of the false pride he had in his own righteousness, and his disgust as he sees it as the rotten rags of Satanic self-love. He declares: "What things were gain to me, those I counted loss for Christ" (vs. 7). Here he is alluding to his "Damascus road" conversion experience. There the truth had first pierced his honest heart like an ox goad. There the contrast between his own hate and rage and the glory and rapture on the face of Stephen, the battered but forgiving martyr, had been clearly revealed. There, on the Damascus road, in a blinding flash Paul had seen that same supernatural love in the face of the ascended Jesus, who spoke to him not in wrath or retaliation but in loving appeal: "Saul, Saul, why persecutest thou Me? Don't you know I love you?" There he had exchanged the rags of his self-loving self for the eternal gain of Christ's own garment of self-giving self.

But then Paul made a startling and costly discovery: The ascended Jesus, now a marvelous Savior to him, was *much more* to him. Christ made it plain that He had come to take over Paul's whole life and express His own love-selfhood through Paul. "Yea doubtless," continues Paul (vs. 8), "I count all things but loss for the excellency of the knowledge of Christ Jesus *my Lord*...." This was something altogether more revolutionary and advanced than merely Jesus as his Savior and Justifier, marvelous though that was. Now this One is to manage his whole life—take him over—so that Paul becomes an embodiment of Jesus Christ *formed in him* as well as *revealed to him.* And this Paul "jumped into"! Everything earthly must go to the winds for that, whatever the cost. There was pain in it: "... for whom I have suffered the loss of all things." There had been the painful cutting-off from all his ambitions as a leading young Jew of his day, with a great future among his own people. This was the paying of the "disciple price," where we hate father, mother, wife, children, houses, lands, physical well-being, and in fact, "*all* that we have," to be a disciple. Paul paid that, and at that time *it was a sacrifice.* And this conditioned Paul for his great Galatians 2:20 revelation, which was his unique contribution to the body of Christ through all the coming centuries. This was Paul as a "young man" (1 John 2:13), in the second stage where he now found himself—which meant finding Christ as the exchanged self in him.

Now comes the most revolutionary change of attitude. He suddenly says that the things it "cost" him to surrender would now be a stench in his nostrils to retain! What was once precious is now disgusting to him. What he had called "suffering the loss of all things" he now says he counts as "stinking dung"! "I count them but dung, that I may win Christ . . . . " A total reversal. And why? Because he was no longer concerned with getting his own inner need settled. This was now completed in Christ—not only Christ *for* him, but now Christ *in* him, *as* him. Now he's free to be one with whom Christ would delight to share His inner self and His purposes. A great ambition had seized Paul—to "win Christ." "Winning Christ" means not depending on Christ for my own convenience any longer but being privileged, rather, to reach a place where He can share with me as His *companion, bosom friend,* and *intimate cooperator* what He came down on earth to do. And how supreme this ambition is! But it is not attained through any methods of the flesh, but only through "the faith of Christ." For Paul continues: " . . . and be found in Him, not having mine own righteousness, which is of the law, but that which is through the faith of Christ, the righteousness which is of God by faith" (vs. 9).

Then Paul explains what these highest ways "in Him" are: "That I may know Him, and the power of His resurrection, and the fellowship of His sufferings, being made conformable unto His death . . . . " To thus "know Him" means an inner understanding of His ways as the Savior: living by the power of His resurrection, as a heavenly man in every earthly condition or daily demand, as Jesus did; fellowshiping with Him also in His sufferings, not now the joys of union but in Jesus' costly identification with the world in its needs, as well as meeting its antagonism. Finally, it means pouring out one's life, not in some quiet retirement, but in God's appointed way—spiritually or physically dying that others may live. This Paul now embraced and lived out in his co-saviorhood, right to its last limit and into its final glory. As he wrote, "... if by any means I might attain unto the resurrection from among the dead" (literal Greek). In this he did not refer, of course, to his share in the bodily resurrection (which is a gift of God to all believers) but to a death like that of Jesus which brings resurrection to others—that "bringing many sons to glory" for which the Captain of our salvation tasted death (Heb. 2:10).

To gain *this*—that by his dying many should live—Paul, now in his old age, pressed toward the mark in that high calling. As he wrote, "Not as though I had already attained, either were already perfect; but I follow after, if that I may apprehend that for which also I am apprehended of Christ Jesus." He lived to take hold of that for which Christ had taken hold of him. People often mistakenly interpret this saying of Paul's as if he wasn't perfect in the sense of sanctification, not yet in the full victory life, and had yet to attain that one day. Not so. Paul had long passed through that second, "young man" stage of handing his whole life over to the Lordship and indwelling of Christ. That was settled forever, as with us who now know *our* second stage. But here he was in his co-saviorhood with Jesus ... who Himself had also said that He had "a baptism to be baptized with; and how am I straitened till it be accomplished!" As Jesus cried out triumphantly on the cross, "It is finished," Paul also in his final letter to son Timothy, when facing his execution, wrote, "I have fought a good fight, I have finished my course"—the glorious course of a gained intercession. Paul the father, Paul the co-priest, Paul carrying right through the purpose for which he was seated in the heavenlies in Christ... yes, Paul the corn of wheat sown in the ground and dying, and bringing forth much fruit.

Now we see what this third level means in our own experience, and that it is to be taken seriously as a *third crisis* of faith and experience. As seriously as the first and second crises. The key scripture summoning us from the second level, to move into the third, is Paul's Romans 12:1: "I beseech you therefore, brethren, ... that ye present your bodies [as] a living sacrifice." (For intercession involves the body, as we shall see later.)

The second stage had been thoroughly established with its final triumphant shout of "no separation"—no separation possible from our eternal union. Paul's "Who shall separate us from the love of Christ?... I am persuaded that [nothing] can separate us... " (Rom. 8:35–39). But now a shock! There is a new and glorious reversal from "no separation" to a voluntary separation from God if necessary—even going to hell that our brother humans may be saved. For Paul immediately thereafter writes about his "great heaviness" for his own people: "I could wish myself accursed [i.e., separated] from Christ for my brethren." This was Paul the intercessor, and it is as such that he calls on us all—all who are redeemed—to present our bodies now as living sacrifices on the altar of *self-giving for others*. While death works in *us*, life will come to *them*. And from this point on in his Roman letter, nothing is spoken about except how the light and life of Christ reaches out *by us* to the world, and how we thankfully use the various gifts with which the Spirit has equipped us—about eighteen in all.

What this means is a total move over, by the compulsion of the Spirit, to a life of unceasing love-activities in spirit and body—from the discipleship to the apostleship level, from the apprenticeship to the proficiency level, from the school of faith to the life of faith . . . yet all (as ever) on the "can't help it" level, with all the zest of living, the enthusiasm, the gaiety-at-heart of a permanent seriousness, where "the zeal of God's house" has eaten us up.

So this is as much a total entry into a fully meaningful relationship with Christ on this *third level* as was the entry into the "replaced life." It is entering into the final and total meaning of our portion of suffering in this life. From the suffering in our sin condition, to the suffering in our striving condition, to the suffering in our self-giving condition. It is revolutionary—and to those not settled and at home with the Trinity in our union relationship, it will again appear blasphemous—because we are really now saying that we are co-gods with God, just as the man Jesus said this to the Pharisees opposing Him (John 10:34–35).

So we see how we have now been permitted to share in the true purpose of sonship: no longer just the privilege of fallen sinners being sons and brothers with the Son, but joining with the Father in His eternal love-purposes for the "final reconciliation of all things," when He'll be known as "God all in all." But if that is glorious for us, it is also most serious; for it means that as sons in this present moment of history, we are co-saviors, co-intercessors, in completing the number of His elect, co-laborers with Him in the harvesting. That also means co-sufferers with Him in "filling up that which is behind [i.e., still lacking] of the afflictions of Christ . . . for His body's sake" (Col. 1:24).* We're on the saving level with Him, and boldly accepting ourselves as such, carrying out the details of His plans, pressing toward the mark, paying the price, and "knowing that our labor is not in vain in the Lord."

*See pages 235-238 and 281.

Chapter Thirty-three

From Disciples to Apostles

But what does this actually mean to us individually? It means that we recognize that we never again have any other meaning to our lives except *His loving others by us*. For as He is the God of love and thus the total self-giver for His universe, so are we. We no longer regard our lives from the aspect of our own convenience, or pleasant or unpleasant situations or relationships, not even our physical well-being. This is the outcome of what was settled within us on our discipleship (learning) level. Jesus had to speak of that in drastic terms to awaken us from any comfortable tendencies to drift along with the tide. He had to say it shockingly: "If any man . . . hate not his father, mother, wife, children, brethren, sisters, yea, and his own life also, he cannot be My disciple" (Luke 14:26). Hold hard! What can that mean? How could Jesus say that? He said it like that to shock us into thinking it through. It seems so wrong, and even ridiculous, that we are forced to ask, What did He mean? It can't mean that! But when we do think it through, we see that all that ever motivated us in our unsaved days was self-love. Our love of others was really only to satisfy our self-love. *My* father, *my* mother, *my* wife, *my* children. The "my" was the real thing to us, not the "them." The *me, my, mine* is all I had. And it is "me"—not the loved ones—that I hate when I come to Christ. Then when I have come, and He to me, the miracle is that the *me, my, mine* is changed to *you* and *yours.* I am now a you-lover, not a me-lover. And now I have the kinsmen all back—to love them, rather than to be loved by them.

But wait a minute—something has happened! Though we do have them back to love and serve them, an inner cutoff has taken place in which we really love *only One* and are joined to One, and our loves for others are secondary expressions of our one love. It is no longer God first and others second. No, it is God only, and all others we love as forms of Him. There is a detaching here which will certainly bring opposition, and maybe persecution, from some loved ones who feel—and rightly so—that they are replaced in the center of our hearts by our Eternal Lover. But during our disciple days, let's be careful. Again, it is not by works: it's not that we "try" to cut ourselves off from anything or anybody. No! *He* does the cutting off, and all He does is always beautiful; and, of course, it does not result in less concern for our loved ones but in more total concern for them to become the total people they really will be in Christ once they come to know Him, though meanwhile our attitude may appear to them as hate or neglect. Neither do we cut ourselves off from the normal way in which God provides our material security, by our jobs or investments. But in His own way *He* does an inner cutting off, by which we know *Him* as our true source of supply. Even if our employment or financial securities are taken from us, we only praise

Him because He is giving us our chance of proving His faithfulness according to His Matthew 6:31-33 word about taking no anxious thought about food or clothing, but rather, "seek ye first the kingdom of God and His righteousness, and all these things shall be added unto you." Many of us have proved that through the years. But again, remember, it is *He* who lovingly loosens us from all earthly ties . . . until by the Spirit we've taken that "flight from the alone to the Alone." He will certainly do it, because He must have us for our eternal destiny as *sons expressing the Father in His Father-nature of love,* and in which alone you and I can find our heart and life's delight. But He always has His own clever ways, so that what we might fear turns out to be a joy and blessing. For *all* is "for His good pleasure," and what He enjoys He will see to it that we also enjoy.

You should read the life of Rees Howells,* the Welsh intercessor, to see a perfect example of how God turns a disciple into an apostle. He got Rees Howells point by point, to the place where the Holy Ghost had no rival in his life, until He had him finally fitted-out for his great life's ministry of intercession.

So we see that there must be a serious weighing-up of our position on the third level, just as there has been on the first and second. We "count the cost," as Jesus said. We need to face the fact that it means that we don't assess life any more on the grounds of What do I get out of it? What happens to me? or Will I achieve what I'm meant to be? And when things "happen" to us in life, we no longer may say "Why this?", as if implying we have been hardly done by.

***Rees Howells, Intercessor*, published by the Lutterworth Press, England, and distributed in the U.S.A. by the Christian Literature Crusade.

No! We see it all in terms of His fulfilling some love and saving purpose *for others* through it, even though at the moment we cannot see that in it.

While that is the negative side of this third-level life, the positive is tremendous—so tremendous that it appears fantastic to our human sight. The positive is what Jesus taught about the Spirit's filling. It is not simply that we thirsting ones may fully drink of Him and remain filled, but Jesus says, "Stretch your believing further. The Holy Spirit didn't come merely to fill *you*; but from *your* fullness *others* will be filled." In other words, He is in you now as rivers of living water *flowing out from you.* This is Jesus' fantastic statement in John 7:38: "He that believeth on Me . . . out of his inmost center shall flow rivers of living water." John, in verse 39, points out that because Jesus spoke this before the Spirit was poured out on all believers at Pentecost, therefore the "shall" has been fulfilled and now *is*!

But out of us will never flow these rivers if we forget our union reality and look at ourselves in our humanity. It then becomes a joke. "Rivers—through me?" But once again, there is only the one way—faith. "He that believeth on Me." So we are right back where we started. Of course, again that "takes the heat" off *us*. "Jesus can save me, a sinner?" Yes! Just transfer your believing to Him and you are saved. "He can deliver me from the efforts of my striving self?" Yes! Just reckon yourself as dead to sin and risen in Him, and now He replaces that spirit of error in you. "There can be rivers of living waters flowing through me?" Yes! Drop your negative believing in your weak little self, stuck away in your small, local situation . . . and look to Him who said that rivers *are* flowing through those who are believing.

I took my first step into that third level (of John 7:38) as a young man, when starting out on my call to the Congo. I was so hesitant, and it seemed so absurd that rivers of the Spirit could flow out of me, that, though I did believe, I was a bit like the man who said to Jesus, "Lord, I believe; help Thou mine unbelief." So I said, "Lord, I believe this word, at least for a muddy trickle to flow out!" But I did believe! And He has surely done more than I asked or thought! So BELIEVE—which is not one whit different from the believing in John 3:16 for salvation and in Galatians 2:20 for oneness. Stand there, laughing, maybe—as I did—at the absurdity of its ever being fulfilled. But remember: faith is substance!

I hope that I have made it plain that the full entry by faith into this apostleship level is definitely a crisis experience involving a fixed inner knowing, as with the other two. Even so, it is true that when we came to Christ we began to be other-lovers and intercessors and witnesses, from our new birth onward. We might say that was the "muddy trickle" stage!

But we are now, again, speaking of something *total*, from which we don't look back, which becomes as fixed in us as did the other two. We *are* now fathers, apostles, bondslaves, co-laborers, co-saviors, intercessors—and the Spirit seals it to us. It requires of us that kind of serious "counting the cost" that Jesus spoke of in Luke 14:28. It is the taking up of our cross voluntarily (and for keeps), just as there was our coming *to* the cross, and then the taking of our place *on* the cross. This is now the cross-bearing for others.

I thank God that it was serious for Pauline and

me. In our engagement days He was working in my heart in that direction, and He had to work on hers to seal it to us both. She got frightened when, perhaps unwisely put, I told her on one occasion, after I had been stirred by reading Charles Finney's *Revival of Religion*, that I had a battle and was alarmed about whether I loved her more than Jesus. So she gave me back the ring, and that really hit me, because what had seemed so clearly of God in our six-month engagement seemed to be completely broken in pieces. But the Lord kept me faithful to my Congo calling, even though in those days we were really only a "family mission" with half a dozen of us living in the Ituri Forest ... and I had to face it, now our engagement was broken, that a friend of mine had his eyes on Pauline and I might find myself in the Congo forest living side by side in the next hut to Pauline and her husband! Then an uncle of mine suggested that I drop going to the Congo and take an opening he offered as a missionary in India. It was a temptation, but I knew God's voice well enough to know that He had called me to the Congo, so I could not turn back. When this news got back to her, she realized that we did love each other and sent an invitation to me to return. I say she proposed to me this time! So we went—and thank God we went! But the main point is that what had bothered her was now settled for both of us. Apparently she had at first said to herself, "If I marry that man, God will be first, God's work will be second, and I'll be third; and I'll be third in no man's life!" But she still is, after sixty years, and I am third in hers. That settled our "apostleship" calling, and it was so serious a settlement that by God's grace we have never gone back on it, and have often renewed it together.

So by one means or another, the Lord will get us fixed as firmly into this third level as He has in the second. If you see this as God's highest and ultimate calling to you, then MOVE IN BY BELIEVING—as you did when you first reckoned on the union, before the realization came. So *believe* and *He will confirm.*

There is one other precious word which fits in with John 7:38. It is Galatians 2:8, where Paul says the Lord is "mighty in me toward the Gentiles." He is in you and me, but now He is mighty, not for our interests, but with a power which will establish Him in others. Mighty—toward the Gentiles. TAKE IT!

Chapter Thirty-four

Not Two Powers—Only One

In what ways does the Spirit flow out of us as rivers? Have we any clear pointers? Yes, there are two. We shall see that He flows out of us as Spirit through spirit (Chapters 34-43) and Spirit through body (Chapters 44-51), and we shall see how He does this.

Let us look into the most basic first: the way He flows out through our spirit. That way, of course, is the way of faith, for the Spirit way is the faith way. We shall be foolish if we think we already know plenty about that way. We have hardly begun! We shall soon find, as I have, that there is plenty more to learn and apply through the whole of life.

The faith way is the one and only way by which the Spirit has flowed into us, and it is the one and only way by which He flows out. As I near the end of my days on earth, I have no more fascinating and fruitful occupation than living the life of faith in action. I join not only with those men of Hebrews 11 in their exploits of faith, but also with great men of faith of my earlier years, such as George Muller and Hudson Taylor, from whom I have eagerly picked up invaluable lessons of faith. But crowning all, for me, have been my years of intimacy with that man of faith and intercession, Rees Howells.

It was not now the faith of my own relationship to God in new birth or union that was interesting me. It was faith applied, and applied effectively, to every incident of my daily life; and beyond that, to the lives and needs of all to whom I was and am sent, or who come to me. This required of me, first, a new expansion to my seeing of things. I had learned that before I can believe, I must see what I am to believe. First, *see*—then *believe*—single sight, then simple faith. But I had *double* sight, and that was my confusion. I saw two powers, good and evil—with plenty of evil. How could I bring the evil within reach of effectively believing God is dealing with it?

So my first step of enlarged understanding was to discover the single eye—to step from seeing *God personal* to *God universal*. It cost me a year to get this finally and completely settled. Thank God, He put me through that painful period. It has altered all my many years—this seeing and knowing how to believe with no weak spots in any situation—and made me able to help others to do the same. As I say, the change didn't depend on the believing, but on the knowing what I could believe. There had to be an expansion of my inner understanding before there could be an expansion of believing.

I first had to have a shock—and this was God's way of shocking me: In the course of my reading, I ran across William James' *Varieties of Religious Experience*. As I read, it seemed to me that he was saying that Paul's conversion was just an inner self-adjustment, not an outward meeting with God on the road to Damascus. I may have misread him, but God meant me to read it like that, for my benefit: a negative to fit me for a total positive! Its effect on me—crazy though it may seem to you of more settled faith—was suddenly to make me wonder whether, after all, there is a human self-sufficiency with no need of God—and perhaps even no God! In other words, I did not have an all-encompassing faith which answered all possible doubts and questionings. But I needed a God with no possibility of a hole in Him.

That sent me on a desperate search. I must have a "total God" or nothing. Indeed, I went so far as to say to God, if there was a God, that I'd had a twenty-year love affair with Him . . . He was all in all to me . . . so if He really was phony and non-existent, I would choose to be phony also, and in my love would cling to Him and be a phony along with Him. Love weathered the storm when the "faith boat" was being rocked. I went through a year's search with much agony of spirit—believing, yet not believing. I need not go into details, except to say that, helped somewhat by the great mystics in their pursuit of and finding union with God, I too finally had a great inner "recognition" that *He is all*. That is why I am so strong on that now His being "all" has meant for me, ever since, that whatsoever there is in the universe, of whatever kind—whether good or evil, negative or positive, including Satan and all his works—God is the source of all, for He is the True All, the Alpha and the Omega. (I am not saying at this moment how that can include evil as well as good, but will explain that shortly.) But it became burned in me like a brand that *I am one with Him in whom the universe is one*. It is like a permanent inner light in me, for He is light . . . and we are light. Some talk of a "cosmic consciousness," and this became that to me, and I am branded.

Chapter Thirty-five

From Negative to Positive Believing

Universal seeing and knowing, with no further double vision—that is what matters. That is the only key to a believing with no kinks in it. While we see Good and Evil as two powers—which was my trouble—we will naturally have a seesaw believing.

The first principle of faith in action, then, is that inner seeing must come before proper believing. Now in this world full of evil and problems, we will always, as humans, start by "seeing things as they are"—as they appear to be—and that means seeing and believing in something that disturbs us, which we call evil, and so it may be. This is "negative" believing . . . and what we are inwardly seeing, and therefore believing, is what we outwardly transmit to others. We can't help it in our looks, words and deeds, for all we share with others is ourselves; and if we see things as evil we transmit negative believing to others—we transmit darkness, not light; death, not life.

Is there an alternative? Yes, there is—and that was what settled into me, once I saw God as all: that there cannot be two powers, for *He* is *one*, absolute and supreme. But how, then, can I include the workings of an evil power, of which the world and people are

From Negative to Positive Believing

so full, as an expression of the one power which is God, who is love?

For that I had to find my solution, and of course I turned to the Bible. There I found the plainest statements, which did link God with evil. The prophet Isaiah said plainly (45:6-7), "I am the Lord, and there is none else. I form the light, and create darkness; I make peace, and create evil [Hebrew *ra*—adversity, calamity]; I, the Lord, do all these things." That statement is total enough. But there are plenty more. To Moses, God said (Ex. 4:11), "Who hath made ... the dumb, or deaf, or the seeing, or the blind? Have not I, the Lord?" When Jeremiah spoke of God's coming judgment on rebellious Israel with the destruction of Jerusalem and the temple, he said that God had called the heathen king who would destroy them "Nebuchadnezzar, *My servant*" (43:10)! The Assyrians God called "the rod of My anger" (Isa. 10:5). All the destructive plagues of insects that destroyed harvest after harvest in the days of Joel the prophet, "the palmerworm, the locust, the cankerworm, the caterpillar," God spoke of as "My great army which I sent among you" (See Joel 1:4 and 2:25). There are dozens of such sayings by the prophets.

We all know about Joseph, and he went even further. He left no room for us to say that God "permits" evil things to happen but does not direct them; for, even though he had suffered thirteen years by being sold as a slave by his brethren and then being thrown into prison because of the false accusation of Potiphar's wife, still he told his brethren, "Ye thought evil against me, but God meant it unto good" (Gen. 50:20). *Meant* it! To "mean" is not to "permit." It is direct purpose and planning.

Peter, in a startling statement in his speech on the day of Pentecost, when referring to the greatest crime in history, told the crowds: "Jesus of Nazareth . . . Him, being delivered by the determinate counsel and foreknowledge of God, ye have taken, and by wicked hands have crucified and slain" (Acts 2:22-23). *Determinate counsel*—there's no possible permissiveness there! And when the believers in those early days of persecution were praying together, they said in their prayer: "For of a truth, against Thy holy child, Jesus, . . . both Herod, and Pontius Pilate, with the Gentiles, and the people of Israel, were gathered together, for to do whatsoever Thy hand and Thy counsel determined before to be done" (Acts 4:27-28). What could be stronger? Jesus Himself, above all, when He stood before Pilate, and Pilate had said "Knowest thou not that I have power to crucify thee, and have power to release thee?", answered, "Thou couldest have no power at all against Me except it were given thee from above"! From above? We would say, if we believed in two powers, "from beneath"!

But Jesus saw only *one power*. At the Last Supper, as Judas left the table to betray Him, Jesus merely said to His disciples, "The prince of this world cometh, and hath nothing in Me." Nothing! Jesus did not see Satan as having any inward footing in Him. And He said the final word when the soldiers were come into the garden to arrest Him, and He told Peter, "Put up thy sword into the sheath; the cup which My Father hath given Me, shall I not drink it?"

And what was that cup? Satan's taking Him to Calvary.

I had the answer to God "meaning evil" when I saw that a person is a *person* only because he is free. Therefore, when God created persons in His own image, they could be persons only by being free, as He is free. And as we have seen manifested in the history of our human family, that had to include our freedom to eat the fruit of the forbidden tree, which in turn had to include its tragic consequences, the sorrows that God in His faithful love told Adam and Eve would come to them. So in creating persons like Himself, who would be free to manage His universe, *they must be free and responsible.* He could do no other, or they would not have been persons. As freedom involves the necessity of making choices, He therefore created them with the possibility of choosing the opposite to Himself, the evil—and they did. In that sense, therefore, God created evil, because, as we have seen, there cannot be consciousness without opposites.

It does not mean that God is the *doer* of that evil. As Paul said, "God forbid!" (Rom. 9:14). And James said, "God cannot be tempted with evil, neither tempteth He any man" (1:13). God does not sin; nor is He responsible when we sin. He created *freedom*, and it is in freedom that there must be this possibility of the alternative choice, and thus in that sense alone He created evil. Satan himself was God's created being, of the highest order. In his freedom he rebelled, and founded the kingdom of darkness of which he is the god. But he is still forever *God's* Satan, and God deliberately used Satan, for instance, to bring Job to the final end of himself (as He uses him in all our lives!). And that is one of the great recorded evidences in the Bible that God is manipulating Satan, not Satan God (Job 1:8 and 2:3). Stretch this out, and (without excusing Satan for his evil designs) we find in all human history we can boldly call Satan "God's convenient agent." We have already sought to make plain that if Satan had not first been free to take us the wrong way, we would never now be safely settled in the right way through Christ. Watch carefully, and see God continually using evil for good purposes: "meaning" the evil as the product of our freedom, but using it for His overcoming grace.

In that sense, then, the Bible says that God "intends" the consequences of evil, whether referring to its corruptions within our personal lives or to all its horrors of disease, disasters, death, cruelties, "man's inhumanity to man." To think that God is taking pleasure in these things, however, is utterly untrue. We know that our fallen, evil condition so pierced His heart that, to redeem us from it, He came in the person of His Son to be perfected in suffering, right up to "tasting death for every man."

But it is necessary that we do recognize that, in another sense, He *does* "mean" evil in all its tragedy, and understand why He means it. Only by that recognition can we be firm and strong—and praising!—when the storms of evil are blowing around us. If, when distressing conditions hit us or our neighbors, we only can say that God "permits it," we seem to imply a weakness in God as if He is sorry about such things but can't help it. However, an element of disturbing incongruity keeps us from ever picturing God as sitting back and leaving the devil free to do his damndest.

So what is the result? When we have these solid grounds for knowing there is *no other way* except that we humans must reap our share of the sorrows of life, and that God *purposes* exactly what has come to us, we then can accept these trials in a totally opposite way—as all joy, instead of all horror. For we know this is the negative background for His great design of perfect love. All is perfect, and He is working out everything "after the counsel of His own will." It is always "the good pleasure of His goodness." And if good and enjoyable to Him, we know it is good and enjoyable to us.

Chapter Thirty-six

Faith in Unlimited Action

What a difference this denouement makes to our normal negative headshaking over all that is happening to us in our personal lives, our families and the world! As we have said, we always start with the negative impact of this world's discords on us, whether in our family life, business, or church relationships. It affects our emotional responses, and we just don't like it. We start with the ever-present temptation to simply believe a thing to be evil—which it is to human eyes. We realize, of course, that we're off-center, because the effect of our negative believing is at once an inner disturbance and darkness. A frown is on our face! We are tempted to quick reactions of temper, impatience, and negative judgmentalism.

By this we learn that, in all problems, the only real problem is ourself. It is our negative believing. What we hold, holds us; and what we are, we transmit. I always know I am off-center when things disturb me. Self-outlook has taken the place of Christ-outlook. When I start that way in my negative human reactions, being tempted to slip back into an independent-self outlook, there is a healthy touch of hell in me.

But now that this wonderful truth has settled into us as total truth—that God is the Lord and there is none else (Isa. 45:5-14), so nothing but what He wills, exists—we know that all these discords are merely disturbed outer conditions, whether in things or people . . . of which the inner center is He. They are disturbed forms of Him and His perfect kingdom of heaven. And now it is simple for us to exchange our negative believing for the positive recognition of God in all. It is surely surprising and humbling to us when we suddenly wake up to how long we have often remained in our negatives!

So now we clearly see that the first way in which rivers of the Spirit flow out of us is in this *reversal of our inner seeing*. We must constantly remember that all we are is spirit, and that all which comes out of us to others is our inner seeings.

We recognize we shall always start with our negative reactions to things or people as they appear to us. We cannot be human and do less. But they are the necessary negative background to Him, the Positive, revealing Himself. We have it now altogether clear that there is none other Lord in the universe but that Perfect One, and that all imperfection is distortion through devil or man—that evil is the misuse of good. And we know that Christ has come to swallow up death with life.

So now we take constant inner practical action. We immediately confront our negative reactions. We recognize them as negative human outlooks which mistake outer appearance for reality. Though hurt by them, perhaps badly and repeatedly, we from our inner center reverse our inner seeing. We die to the human outlook by "bearing about in our body the dying of the Lord Jesus." We cannot change our soul-feelings, but we do change our spirit-attitude. Then we affirm that *all is perfect,* horrible or offensive though it may appear. We always see Him "meaning" that situation—even meaning persons to be in their distorted forms, but with Him at their hidden center. We see only perfect love and perfect power. We see now with heavenly, not earthly eyes. We see as He sees. We count the "divers trials" as all joy. We glory in the tribulation. We believe against appearances, and accept and praise. We repeat this perhaps a thousand times in our daily lives, in things large and small, and it turns the distresses of life into daily adventure. He that sits in the heavens laughs, and we laugh with Him.

And that laughter rings out of us in word and look, and touches our world. "How can this crazy person be happy and thankful in evil circumstances? He's got *something*, crazy or no!" "I wish *I* could be happy and peaceful in *my* depressing conditions." A secret hunger is there. Some come and inquire and ask for help, and we give it to them. We always share what we've got; and some get fed and become feeders of others, and so the rivers flow.

So our faith attitudes give life, even before they become faith actions (which we shall shortly look into) "Keep thy heart with all diligence, for out of it are the issues of life." Daily, momentarily, we keep our inner attitudes God-centered in God's purposes, and life issues from us. This is the pure heart that sees only God, and views all circumstances with Him of whom it is said, "Thou art of purer eyes than to behold evil." It produces the thrill of our daily adventure, and is within reach of us all, in all conditions. Let us remember that nothing outer holds us. We are only held by our own self-attitudes. If we see evil, and are held by our seeing, we have our inner hells of fear, hate, struggle, pessimism. If in all things we see Him who is always perfect goodness, we have our present heaven, and are busy introducing others to it.

Chapter Thirty-seven

Modern Science Helps

Though not directly affecting us, yet it is both encouraging and helpful to take a glance for a moment at the radical changes in the attitude of modern science to the material universe. I do it as an ignorant amateur, but one greatly interested.

We see how great has been the break-up of the old materialistic concepts of a generation ago, with a move over from the material to the immaterial. These concepts don't affect our living faith, which has wholly other foundations, but the startling changes are interesting and greatly intriguing, and we would say *helpful to faith.*

Science has really taken a great leap to a certainty that, as the Bible said long ago, the visible is made out of the invisible. Mass is energy, and matter is really trapped light. The physicists have reached so far these days that they have passed beyond the atom to the sub-atoms, all those mysterious so-called particles; and their remarkable findings are that these can no longer be tied down to being what we would call "material particles," however minute. They can only be described as "events" where there is a conjunction of space and time; and they are moving so rapidly that they can only be spoken of as "patterns of probabilities." They can only be known by their interconnectedness with the whole, and these interconnections are inseparable, so that everything is contingent on the existence of the rest. Thus, for instance, a spin dryer, which by its motion throws out the water from the clothes, only does so "by its relation to the fixed stars"; and if the stars disappeared, the force of the rotating body would disappear also. Thus everything in the universe is interconnected. There is no such thing as empty space. All is filled with dynamic energy, just as much as visible matter is. Indeed, as Einstein said, all are "fields of vibrating energy," and what we regard as matter is "constituted by the regions of space where the field is extremely intense." All is really an unbroken wholeness, and absurd as it sounds to us in our ignorance, "a single particle contains all other particles." With that has come the new recognition, which was the basis of Einstein's relativity theory, that all depends on us, the observers. All is relative to where we stand and how we see a moving thing. There are even suggestions (still more absurd to such as us) that all things are products of the observers, even to the effect that we could influence or change past history as well as future. Fantastic! But is not all this pointing to matter as a product of mind, and don't we believers know Him who is the one Mind of the universe? Does it not also take us nearer to Paul's statement that the whole groaning creation waits to find its deliverance by the manifestation of the sons of God? "For the earnest expectation of the creature waiteth for the manifestation of the sons of God, ... because the creature itself also shall be delivered from the bondage of corruption into the glorious liberty of the children of God" (Rom. 8:19-21). And it was God Himself who "made the creation subject to vanity," with that glorious purpose in view.

Our present interest is that this is showing us that what we used to call "material substance" is altogether broken up today. Researches are going on into what they call a "fourth dimension," where space and time are interrelated in a way beyond our natural understanding. It is in that realm that the true origin of our material universe is found, where all is really energy. For mass is but energy divided by the inconceivable speed of the speed of light multiplied by itself ($M = e/c^2$, or $E = mc^2$). And we are now seeing how all this is being connected with the involvement of the observer with what is observed. It is an approach to the dimension to which *we* have already come, to the dimension of spirit, where Paul said long ago of Christ as Creator: "By Him all things consist [cohere, are held together]" (Col. 1:17), and that God's revealed purpose is "to gather together in one all things in Christ, both which are in heaven, and which are on earth" (Eph. 1:10). The physicist, however brilliant, cannot, with only his natural mind, find ultimate truth through science; truth is a living Person, the living Christ, and He can only be found person to person at the foot of His cross, whether by a Nobel prize-winner or an uninformed layman. But scientists are more allies than opponents in accepting the spiritual as the real when they say that all is really light, "trapped light." For "God is Light."

Chapter Thirty-eight

Speaking the Word of Faith

We have seen that one stream of the rivers of living water flows out from us in our believing attitudes. We might call this the Power of Positive Believing. We have it clear that everyone, with no exception, is projecting his attitude. No man can live unto himself. Modern science informs us that every atomic particle has its field of attraction or repulsion; so also we humans have. The poet Francis Thompson wrote in "The Mistress of Vision":

> All things by immortal power,
> Near or far, hiddenly,
> To each other linked are,
> That thou canst not stir a flower
> Without troubling of a star . . . .

Paul said the same with his "None of us liveth unto himself, and no man dieth unto himself."

We know well enough what our frowns and head-shakings and pessimism and general negative attitudes do. How wonderful it is, instead, to be constant inner-see-ers of God, in His perfect ways, *meaning* everything and everybody to be at this moment just what they are. Thus "with the lift of our soul," without effort or put-on-ness, maybe saying nothing, but with the replacement of the garment of praise for the spirit of heaviness, not trying to impress or change a person, we cannot but be a light of hope, praise, and faith in dark places. We are not hiding the apparent hurts. But mercy is *rejoicing* against judgment in us, and there is no hiding it. The Spirit is secretly touching the strings of response in hearts where there are only the bass notes sounding.

But spirit *attitude* is only the preliminary to spirit *action*. No person on earth functions without first inwardly reacting to things, and is always in a negative or positive attitude toward them. From this he moves on to the moment of decision as to what he will do about it. The general thought-level, which can move in any direction, is now replaced by a decisive, inner word-level. He says within himself, "I will do this," "I will take that," "I will go there." Thus he speaks within himself his "word of faith." From that inner process, by which general thought is replaced by specific word, he now moves on to outer deed— from *thought* to *word* to *deed*. From Father-level to Son-level to Spirit-level. By no other process has any single conscious action ever taken place in all human history. It is the universal human process of self-manifestation, whether it is the taking and eating of some food from a plate, or a decision of the United States Congress! It is also the process of creation in Genesis 1. The Father has His universal plan of the ages; the Son, called the Word, gives the plan its particular form with His "Let there be"; the Spirit moves upon the face of the waters and transforms the word into substance. Father, Son, Spirit—thought, word, deed.

The critical moment of any action, whether by the Three-in-One, or by man made in His likeness, is *the speaking of the decisive word*: attitude (Father) moves into word (Son) and action (Spirit). That is why we say that a word puts a person in action.

In *any* mundane activity, this is the order. Thoughts are preparatory. Deeds are the products. *Speaking the decisive word* transmutes the thought into deed. The *word* is at the heart of the process. So a person in action is really his word in action.

Now move that up into the operations of the kingdom of God, the realm of the spirit dimension, of which all earthly forms are visible reproductions—spirit-essence slowed down to the point of visibility. Now we are the sons of God operating in the Spirit kingdom, though outwardly flesh members of a three-dimensional world. How *then* do we operate? *Precisely as we do in our three-dimensional world of space-time.* Not one iota of difference. We operate from the Father-level of our general understanding of situations and the purpose in them, on to the Son-level of the decisive moment of the spoken word of what is to come to pass, and on to the Spirit-level of the thing done. But how can we say that? Because we as sons of God are in union with the Father, Son, and Spirit by His grace and election; and that union means that we are so inwardly one that *we act as He.* We think His thoughts; we speak His word of faith; we do His deeds.

How do we think His thoughts on the Father-level? Because we have the mind of Christ, as the Scripture states. We no longer look around outside us, or upward, to gather His thoughts. We understand that He is living out His perfect purposes by His body members . . . and therefore by me as one of them. Therefore, whatever situation I am at present in is precisely the expression of His present mind for me. All, then, that I have to do is to sort out in my mind what is the situation in which He is now living by me, and what is my relation to the people with whom He has linked me. This necessitates seeing each situation as His perfect purpose.

But now we go further. I have taken it for granted that He has a distinct purpose to fulfill by me, His son, in the situation. I must now, therefore, *particularize* the circumstances or the people concerned, and know what it is He purposes doing in them. What is that particular thing? I must get that "in the clear" to move on to the decisive word of faith. How do I get it clear? By boldly taking it for granted that He thinks His present thoughts by me. For He is "working in me to will and do of His good pleasure." He is causing me to desire His desires. So I name that desire precisely, for "What things soever ye [not He] desire . . . , ye shall have" (Mark 11:24). I do not hesitate, except for whatever time it takes to formulate my desire. (And if I am part of a group, together seeking the mind of God, it may take a while to get to one mind.) So first comes *attitude*.

Then I move straight in to the Son-level of speaking the word of faith. I do precisely what Jesus (in Mark 11:20-26) told His disciples to do. He had earlier commanded the fig tree to bear no more fruit (vss. 12-14). The next morning, when they passed the withered tree, Peter commented on it: "Master, look, the fig tree you cursed is withered away." Jesus simply replied, "Now *you* have this same 'faith of God'" (which is the literal rendering, rather than "faith in God"). And what does that mean? Obviously, *seeing as God sees the situation,* and thus believing with His believing. And how does God do this? Through my eyes and inner comprehension. So if something appears like a mountain of difficulty to me, that is how He is first causing me to see it.

Jesus then tells His disciples to *say* to any such mountain, "Be thou removed, and be thou cast into the sea," and in doing so, to believe it is a completed fact. The result: "You will have whatever you have said." It couldn't be simpler. Don't beg. Don't beseech. Just *say it*! But there is the added proviso that we don't doubt in our hearts—don't allow mental soul-doubts, which we surely have, to disturb our fixed, inner word of faith: "Whosoever . . . shall not doubt in his heart, but shall believe that those things which he saith shall come to pass, he shall have whatsoever he saith" (vs. 23).

But how can I say "Be removed" to a mountain? Because it is only a mountain to my human seeing. Read what God said to Zerubbabel in Zechariah 4:7: "Who art thou, O great mountain? Before Zerubbabel . . . a plain." Thus to the eyes of faith a "mountain" is no obstacle, and as Jesus said, is removed and cast into the sea by the word of faith.

So, having the mind of Christ, as "sons in action" we discern that "next thing" God is moving us on to and bring it into being. *It is just that simple.* It is only the "graveclothes" of suspicion of our old self-seeking selves which makes us hesitate about saying that the thing we desire is His mind. But He has said, "What things soever ye desire when ye pray, believe . . . " (vs. 24). *You* desire. Then let's be that simple. If He in us trusts our desires to be His desires, let us trust ourselves. We have discarded and rejected those doubtings and questionings of our motives by accepting our vital Galatians 2:20 relationship, so let us now practice holy boldness, just as John keeps saying in His union epistle: "We have confidence toward God . . . . This is the confidence that we have in Him . . . . We may have boldness [even] in the day of judgment."

Then, being bold in defining exactly what are the things we are presently desiring in place of the mountain confronting us, and naming them, we speak the key word of the countdown—we press the button marked, "SAY." We do that from our inner spirit-center, simply by our authority as sons of God. Jesus has plainly told us to act *as God* by "the faith of God"—by His inner believing imparted to us, by our inner union of mind and understanding. This means that in acting as He, all of His mighty resources are at *our* disposal. It is not now a matter of us being at *His* disposal, but of Him being at *our* disposal. He is operating in this present world-system *by us*. We say with Caleb, "Let us go up at once and possess it, for we are well able to overcome it." And in so doing, we laugh the laugh of faith.

Speaking this word of faith (having once settled what the desire is) could not be more simple. It is the "obedience of faith" (Rom. 16:26). That is all the "works" involved. It is a *work* of faith to this extent: all that the outer appearances can pour on us at such a "speaking" moment, they will pour. That is to say, we shall likely feel the full impact of the foolishness of faith. It looks absurd. It *is* absurd, because the agony of faith is that *nothing can ever be experienced until after we've committed ourselves to it, not before.* As we've seen, that is actually true in a minor way of even the least act of everyday faith, like sitting on a chair. *How much more* when it is these leaps into what is invisible and impossible and unattainable by human methods! So there is a travail of faith because of the assaults on us by every emotional reaction to the absurdity and impossibility of it. And equally, by every rational objection to what spirit-faith has always been—the irrational. So in that sense, we say speaking this word is *not simple.* Yet it is, because it is just *speaking the word*! And that is why something equivalent to "confessing it with our mouth" is a seal on it—a means by which, once we have said a thing, it's a settled matter—and the affirmation to ourself or to others helps to settle us into it. But that's all. These are our *supreme moments* when the rivers of the Spirit are flowing out of us on our spirit level. This is the faith that gives substance to things hoped for.

Chapter Thirty-nine

How It Affects Our Prayer Life

Speaking the word of faith obviously makes a big difference to our prayer life. In explaining this new understanding of prayer I have sometimes said that "I don't pray any more." I should not say that, chiefly because the Bible is full of exhortations to prayer and illustrations of prayer. What I'm meaning is that at the heart of my praying, the prayer of request has been replaced by the prayer of acceptance of what I've asked for. Certainly, prayer cannot mean what we often interpret it to mean—having special times of prayer, etc.—because Paul has told us to pray without ceasing, and *that* we *cannot do* unless we see prayer to be a condition in which communion with God is always continuous, on our subconscious (and, as needful, conscious) level.

I am not now referring to those periods of corporate prayer expressing fellowship, worship and praise. Some enjoy them in the quietness of an Episcopal-type worship service, or of the Lord's Supper. Others, including myself, though being most at home in home fellowships, also enjoy the Spirit-led out-pourings in more charismatic-type meetings when all are unitedly and vocally pouring out their hearts in praise; and this may often include both songs and singing in the Spirit, in one great volume of sound, sometimes interspersed with messages in tongues and interpretations. This was obviously part and parcel of the normal worship times in the early church (1 Cor. 14:26-33). It shows how far we have cooled off from the glow and freedom of those days when, in our established churches, we have a pastor to do the praying and preaching. This is a far call from a fellowship so living, and with so many wanting to take part, that it isn't a question of calling on and encouraging the brethren to participate but rather of having enough orderliness for one to follow another, and giving room for two or three to speak in tongues also.

How far we've come when such a message in tongues would cause a shock (and even division) in the church fellowship, instead of being so ordinary that no notice is taken. I was in a fellowship I like to be with in Halford House, Richmond, England, on a Sunday morning, with about two hundred present. In the freedom of the worship hour I heard one speak in tongues with an interpretation. Then another spoke and no interpreter. When I inquired afterwards about the one with no interpretation . . . "You made a mistake," said my friend. "The second one was a Chinese sister speaking in her own language." But the point I am making is that in a period of worship and praise by song, prayer, Scripture, a message in tongues may be taken for granted; and it was a non-Pentecostal assembly. How far we have wandered.

It is something to hear the rising and falling of the sound of the Spirit in a Korean country congregation, maybe of a couple of thousand—and Presbyterian—

unitedly praying at 4:00 a.m.; and that glow and glory can be shared today in many fellowships of many natures, by no means officially Pentecostal.

But back to our main line about the word of faith as the heartbeat of our prayer life. We have seen that we first need to know the mind of Christ, in each given situation, *expressed through our own minds*—relating to the challenge, the mountain that confronts us. Knowing that His mind and ours are in union, we come to a plain settlement (even if it takes time to sort things out) of what it is that *we* desire in the situation. We then boldly take it for granted that that means *His* desire *by us,* knowing that He freely said in Mark 11:24, "What things soever *ye* desire, when ye pray, believe that ye receive them, and ye shall have them."

And now we are moving into the heart of the matter. Jesus had just said, "*Say* unto this mountain, Be thou removed . . . " and you will have whatsoever you say. Now, speaking of naming our desires in prayer, He said, "*Believe* that you have received them, and they shall be granted you"—"*have received,*" not "receive"—and I quote the *New American Standard* version here, because it best brings out the meaning of the Greek aorist tense.

This is where the difference lies between my former request-type praying and what Jesus was saying to His disciples and now us. I see God marvelously privileging me and you to be *His agents of production* in lives and conditions. Just as we produce in the material realm by specifically deciding what we shall make and then making it, so now in the realm of the Spirit. For me, I ask no longer, unless I also believe and receive.

Folks say, "But doesn't God tell us to ask?" Yes, but asking is not to inform God of what I need. "Your heavenly Father knoweth that ye have need of all these things," said Jesus. What *is* required is God getting me in my childish ignorance to the point of deciding what He is meaning me to ask for. Just as you get a child to choose which cookie he will take and then ask for just that one. So asking is just a stepping stone to receiving. As Jesus said, "Ask . . . seek . . . knock, and it shall be opened unto you." So to my asking I add taking and receiving. Indeed, as I get used to taking by the word of faith, I hardly notice I'm asking—one is almost dissolved into the other.

So I move right in and speak the desire into reality. How? By that word of faith which "calls the things that be not as though they were," which is said to be God's form of faith (Rom. 4:17), and therefore mine. I speak that word. When it is on the mundane, human level that I speak any such word, *I* then go on to fulfill it. This time I am recognizing that it is *God* speaking that word by me, and so *He* goes on to fulfill it—and it is precisely the same as when He brought the visible creation into being by the word of His Son.

Chapter Forty

A Faith Illustration

I learned the speaking of the word of faith as a regular principle of life through my friend Rees Howells. I listened to him in his daily talks on how the men of God in the Bible came to the point of speaking that word of faith. It gradually soaked into me that this was not some occasional, rather exotic way of handling life's challenges, but the normal one. I saw it in the men of the Bible, and supremely in the life of Jesus Himself. Moses announced the ten plagues to Pharaoh one by one, crossed the Red Sea, got water from the rock, assured the people of daily manna... each by some specific word, such as "Stand still, and see the salvation of the Lord which He will show you today; for the Egyptians whom ye have seen today, ye shall see them again no more forever. The Lord shall fight for you, and ye shall hold your peace"—when the Israelites were terrified by the chariots of Pharaoh pursuing them. Joshua, when the priests blew the trumpet, commanded the army around Jericho: "Shout, for the Lord hath given you the city"; David declared to Goliath, "This day will the Lord deliver thee into my hand"; Elijah told

Ahab, "There shall not be dew nor rain these years but according to my word."

Those great Bible examples could seem out of reach to us ordinary twentieth-century folk. But I observed Rees Howells at his Bible College put faith into present-day action. And I have since seen multitudes of instances of this during my years in the Worldwide Evangelization Crusade.

I had, as a young man, joined C.T. Studd in the heart of Africa, after my army years in World War I and a time at Cambridge. I had been attracted by his new venture, then called the Heart of Africa Mission, because it was founded on the principle that God alone would be the supplier of all needs . . . according to His promises, with no appeals made to man, and no needs mentioned except to God. The Crusade has remained wholly faithful to this principle these sixty-eight years of its existence. Pauline and I lived like this with C.T. Studd and our fellow workers in the Belgian Congo, and experienced God's faithfulness.

Meanwhile, back in Britain I had become a close friend of Rees Howells, and the first link between us was his sense of oneness in spirit with C.T. Studd, whom he had never met. From Rees Howells I learned not just an almost unnoticed walk of faith regarding the daily supplies coming from God, but a principle of faith to be definitely applied to *every* challenging circumstance of life, the way Jesus plainly acted in meeting every variety of need.

My Waterloo came when C.T. Studd in the heart of Africa was "glorified" (the way we always speak of the "death" of God's servants), going to the Lord in 1931 with "Hallelujah! Hallelujah!" as his last words. He had commissioned Pauline and me to return to the home base in England and carry on the Crusade with the thirty-five workers in the Congo, and just we two at home. That first month at home we received $500 for those workers for a month! And it was precisely then, at the bottom of a dry well, as it were, that I looked up to the glimmer of light at the top and was challenged to put into practice on my own what I had learned from others.

I am writing this not from any special interest in the incident, but because it illustrates what we are talking about—*how to use the word of faith*. The way we then did it is the way I and so many others still do it today. Not one iota of difference. That is why I mention it in detail: as an example of practicing the faith way as the *only* way—the only *workable* way—of living, applicable to every detail of our lives. For though learned, perhaps, in a crisis, it is then to be practiced in all our daily situations.

There were four of us together one day at the house which was our London headquarters in 1931. There was Pauline and I, one missionary recruit, and one missionary on furlough. What did we do? First we faced our negatives. Things were at the collapsing point: Trouble had arisen and many had left us. The Depression had hit and money was practically nonexistent. We had plenty of advice to "give up"— close the small mission, or offer it to others. (This situation was of the same kind that we are all confronted with at times, with pressing, even disastrous negatives: What shall I do about this mountain, this hopeless situation, this impossible person?)

Well, I had learned the first step from Rees Howells. Not calling on God and asking Him for deliverance; nor listening to man—but listening to God. In other words, not what *we* think about it, but what has *He* to say to us about it. "What's up, God?" This is revolutionary (and has remained so) because it reverses prayer. It is not we talking *to Him* and bringing Him our needs, but giving Him the chance to talk *to us*.

For us at that time it certainly was the difference between collapse and continuing. We listened. But how does God talk to us, or we hear His voice? We have already gone into that: by knowing our inner spirit-union, then catching on to what comes to our minds as what He is saying to us. On that occasion, a thought came to us fully suitable to our special calling. We remembered that our founder, when he first went alone as a pioneer to the heart of Africa, wrote that God had spoken to him on board ship "in strange fashion" and said to him, "This journey is not only for the heart of Africa but for the whole unevangelized world." He had added, when he wrote this home to his wife, "To human reason it sounds ridiculous, but faith laughs at impossibilities and cries, 'It shall be done!'"

Well, that was certainly absurd to us. Our thirty-five in the Congo were almost at starving level, and here God was coming back to us through our founder and saying, "Not only for the heart of Africa but for the whole unevangelized world." But we knew it was the word of the Lord in all this impossibility, and we accepted it. For C.T. Studd had said specifically: "Faith laughs at impossibilities," and this was where he and Rees Howells talked the same language—faith!

So the next thought that came to us—His mind in our mind (We were not doing any official praying, not on our knees. We were sitting talking, and this was our prayer!)—was, What does "faith" mean when it comes to a matter not of theory but of action? That led us to the Bible, which was always our foundation—the Bible interpreted to us by the Spirit. It seemed practical to us to turn to the experience of Joshua, for he was Moses' successor . . . and in a minute way we were successors to our Moses, C.T. Studd. So we read Joshua chapter one, and that was where God's mind speaking through our minds put us right into focus, put us right along the lines Rees Howells had always talked about and showed us in his own life. We read how God spoke to Joshua and told him to pick up the torch that Moses had laid down and go forward into the promised land, crossing the Jordan River.

Well, that was still theory to us. Exhortation wasn't what we needed. It was how to get into action. So we read further. That interview with God closed with verse 9. Then the paragraph mark: change of subject. And here was our key illumination—a lifelong one to me. We read that Joshua called together the officers of his army and told them to make practical preparations—commissariat, food, etc.—for Joshua said, "Within three days ye shall pass over this Jordan." That was what struck us. By what authority did Joshua name "three days" and then say with total confidence that they would *then* cross the flooded river? God had not said that to him.

Then we saw. We got into focus how Joshua and all such men spoke their words of faith. They named their needs. *They*, not God. "What things soever *ye* desire." This was the secret. The hidden key. This life is not to be we men pathetically depending on God,

A Faith Illustration

calling on God as though at a distance and not too willing to help. It is God's marvelous plan of entrusting Himself to man, joining Himself to man as man. It is man speaking as God. It is union in action, just like with Moses, Elijah, and the rest. It was Joshua who, as a military commander, calculated the days needed for preparation and then fixed a timetable by the word of faith. He had got it! He understood that God had entrusted His own plans and the power for their fulfillment to His anointed agents—which we all are. *You define what you need and how much you need. Then you say so.* That's all. You say it is coming. That it is there already in your sight. "Within three days ye shall pass over."

It is always our speaking our word of faith which puts a person into action. But this is not human action. It is God-action, Spirit-action, and the river will dry up and the people cross. So we see that all hangs on this spoken word of faith, and that's all; because it really is God the Father speaking His word by His son or daughter, through whom the Spirit then moves into manifestation. Do we see this?

We did that morning. We sat together and spoke that word. We calculated our "three days" to be that God would start sending new recruits, the first of a great army, to fill gaps in the Congo as well as going to other lands. (We took no note of the needs of the existing workers, for we knew that was God's normal business.) We named "ten," and that as the first token of a world-wide advance to begin in the Congo. They would come in a year, by the first anniversary of C.T.'s glorification. We said it, named the number, and the day—July 16, 1932—and used that scripture we have already quoted in Mark 11:24. We believed we had received, as it says.

Next day as we gathered, one of us asked the Lord to remember and send the ten. The Spirit rebuked us. Do you ask for what you've got? If you got it yesterday, shouldn't you give thanks? So for the rest of that year—no man knowing what was happening—we thanked, watched, and often laughed, as the ten came: called (with Bible-school training), financed, and commissioned to the Congo where they all went. The last one, Ivor Davies, was given the name *Kumi* in Africa, which means "ten." The last £200 needed for his passage there came three days before the anniversary. We were in Belfast, in a prayer conference which began five days before, watching each mail, and the telegram came from Pauline in London: "200 pounds for the ten, Hallelujah." We heard later that it had come from two old ladies whom we had never met. So thank God for old ladies!

The next year we moved on to fifteen, the next twenty-five, the next fifty, the next seventy-five—and they came. There would be no point in giving further details, for we are looking at principles. But I thank God that the Worldwide Evangelization Crusade, coupled with the Christian Literature Crusade (which was born out of it), together have some 1500 workers, establishing the gospel in over forty fields. Thank God, today thousands around the world have confessed Christ and are themselves now forming national churches, spreading the gospel witness. The whole company of Crusaders are still living with enthusiasm on the promises of God, applying these same principles of faith to all kinds of advances.

Millions of dollars now come in annually . . . when it was but five thousand that first year. I do not mean to disregard the fact that there have been failures en route. And trials. For some there has been the glory of martyrdom, as they have laid down their lives for Christ. There are objectives of faith not yet in the visible; but on the whole, we have seen overwhelming evidences of the truth of God's word—that "faith is the substance of things hoped for, the evidence of things not seen."

Chapter Forty-one

What if It Doesn't Happen?

Now the question is, Does this illustration bring home to us the fact that faith is consummated in our word of faith? For third-level living requires a catching on to the mind of God through our minds in a situation, replacing our negative thinking; then boiling it down to a clear, specific objective; then stating that objective in its direct, practical form by my word of faith; then believing that it is already in existence, because there is no time factor (past, present or future) in God's "fourth dimension." So we also, as He, call the things that be not as though they are.

Then, having done that by our word of faith, we never repeat it again in the form of a request; we don't ask, we thank. We continue repeating our "thank you" in our inner recognition of what is coming, for our faith has within it a "sense" of the thing anticipated. We already "see" in faith as well as speak that word of faith.

Never, of all things, do we ask, "Why hasn't it happened?" We surely give ourselves totally away, if, when the answer has not yet come (or even after it "cannot" come, for the time for the answer has passed with no answer) we say, "He hasn't done what I believed for. It hasn't happened. Faith doesn't work." By that we would imply that the answer depended on our faith, and this has failed; or we have believed amiss, or something. But it is *His* faith expressed by us, and we are saying *He has done it.* Not we, but He. Therefore, if it is a done thing by the word of faith, we never say it hasn't been done. Never! For our word of faith means that we have said it has happened in the spirit. It *has happened,* and if someone says it hasn't happened, we *still* say it has happened. God will fulfill His own word. It was He who told us to say to that mountain "Be gone!" and to believe that, when we pray, we have received. So *it has happened.* Hold on! Even if we do not see things until the other side of the grave! For it was said of the men of faith in Hebrews, "These all died in faith, not having received the promises but having seen them afar off, and were persuaded of them, and embraced them." But even if they did not receive the fullness, they did have a good slice of the cake en route! I believed God for a solution to a problem in our missionary work forty years ago. I expected the answer, but did not see it come, and was tempted to say, "No answer. I must have been mistaken." But just *now* the answer is appearing.

Of course the temptation is to question. "Was it my faith at fault?" "Was my motive right?" "Was I mistaken or presumptuous in speaking that word of faith?" Never accept those questionings which come from our souls. They come from the recurring temptation to move back into "separation"—as if it is not God speaking by us in our fixed union, but that we still have our separate, self-condemning selves.

Condemnation accompanied by darkness comes from beneath. Conviction accompanied by light and peace comes from above. Go back to our spirit-centers where the word is "Be still, and know that I am God." If I totally trust Him with a single eye, I shall see that what appeared to me to be a mistake, or to have had some flesh motivation behind it, is not; God will give the perfect and fully satisfying fulfillment. Such times, when apparently faith does not become substance, are given us to establish us more thoroughly in the fact that we have the mind of Christ and must not recognize the false possibility that we are back in our old, divided, self-motivated outlook.

As for "presumption," what that really means is that my word of faith had behind it a desire for my own satisfaction or self-display, rather than being solely for the glory of God or the benefit of others, or perhaps was meant to test God's faithfulness. Don't be frightened by such a barb. Don't accept that in our union relationship with Christ our motives are flesh-centered. Stand to your "launch out in faith," and believe that God meant it.

Sometimes, as with Paul, the exact desire, as first named, is refused: not with a *No* but with a far vaster *Yes*. Because if Paul had gotten the removal of his thorn in the flesh, we should all have forgotten about that as an incident of history. But we never forget the answer he received—a support to the whole church of Christ in all of the pressures of life—that "God's strength is made perfect in weakness" (2 Cor. 12:7-11). And so inwardly conscious of this did Paul become that he went on to say, "Therefore I take pleasure in infirmities, in reproaches, in *necessities*, in persecutions, in distresses for Christ's sake"; and then, no longer mentioning God in it, " . . . for when I am weak, then am *I* strong." That is *union*. That is Paul *speaking and living as God*. A far vaster answer for the centuries than a temporary healing. So here it is. Keep speaking the word of faith, as I do, all the time. Say again and again, "This has happened, that has happened, for I inwardly see it *has* happened." Watch for the happening, and enjoy the many times you see it happen.

By now it is surely clear that this is radically different from the normal underlying faith by which all who are born-again live. In that sense all Christians walk by faith and not by sight. But on the third level, "father" grade, of which we are now speaking, faith is the operating agent, the one and only means by which every situation of life is authoritatively handled. We are mountain-movers. Like those in Hebrews 11, we are stopping the mouths of lions; out of weakness we are made strong. We have an appetite for "tight corners," as C.T. Studd said, to "give us the luxury of seeing God deliver us out of them." We are now in permanent faith-action, as Jesus was on earth. This is the commissioned third-level life, using the word of faith as naturally and continually as we make normal human decisions. It is our common habit and practice.

We say this to underline that *third-level living—* with the rivers flowing outward, with the Spirit "mighty in us" towards all—means *life is constant faith-action,* way beyond the normal way of life in which, on occasions, prayer or faith is a useful resource. On this level, *all* life is faith-in-action. We are "fathers in action."

Chapter Forty-two

Difficult People

Then there is the matter of loved ones. How many carry burdens for loved ones unsaved or backslidden. We cry day and night like the importunate woman calling on the unjust judge. But suppose we kind of "gather up our garments about us" and speak the word of faith: "It is done." We know that we *should* do this because we can have what we want. Well, *do it*! *By faith* see God at work in that precious one, beneath all the appearances of sin and flesh and maybe antagonism and contempt. Don't see him or her in those fleshly appearances. See him as a precious and loved son of God, though still a prodigal son. See him as a marred son of God, just as I was—prodigal, but a *son*. Tell him you have seen him in your faith and that God will get him, for he *is* His. And see all the positives you can in his life, which you can appreciate and for which you can be thankful.

Always remember our true perspective: God is the All in all. Therefore, when I am confronted with this or that situation it is *He* who put me there, and I know why: He is going to come through with some new and glorious manifestation of Himself—the positive through the negative. He only works through His sons, and in this case He is telling me, "I am going to do it *through you.*" My hurt and disturbance is His way of stirring me to move into my word of faith. That is why in Isaiah there is that upside-down statement, "Before they call, I will answer" (65:24). "No," we would say. "Call first on the phone and then get the answer. Not answer before call!" But God already has the answer—and He has in me a son whom He can trust not to be knocked down by the problem, but to turn it into a call on Him; and my way of calling will be my word of faith ... and through the faith will come the substance. Indeed, He deliberately puts me in my "hot spots" to cause me to want deliverance, and to speak that deliverance-word of faith. That is how He finds me—and you—to be a profitable son.

That loved one *is* saved. We may have often to repeat that to ourself or to others, when nothing seems changed. But we repeat it—not the prayer of request, but the word of faith. What burdens that takes off our heart, and how it changes our attitude toward the one we have believed for, because we practice seeing through to who he is by the eyes of faith, rather than being obsessed by the unpleasant present appearances; and *our change of attitude is what God uses to change him,* for beneath the facade of defense there is really a hungry, watching heart. And by taking such positions of faith for those nearest to us, we then are ourselves freed to reach out in faith for others. St. Augustine, when he found the Lord after his dissolute life, asked his mother where he had been all those years. "In my faith and love," she answered.

When someone asks me to pray with them for a loved one, maybe a husband or wife, I say briefly to her (supposing it's a wife), "It isn't your husband who is the problem. You are the problem. You as a daughter of God have the right to speak the word of faith that God *has* your loved one saved or delivered." I give her the scriptures and the promises. Then I say, "I won't pray for you more than this one time. But if you like—and you see that you have this right to believe—I will join you now in your word of faith." That is much more help to her than my just praying a prayer with her. It is helping her to be the wife of faith.

And if someone says, "But how can you say by faith that God has your loved one saved? Hasn't he a will of his own?", my answer is that *his will is not what controls him.* It is his *wants*, and *his will will follow his wants.* And God has His own clever way of changing our wants. He can make us sick of what we used to want from this world, and can make us want *Him.* Then our will will follow our want.

Our relationship to our fellow Christians radically changes also, when we know who we are, for then we know who *they* are. I first see my brother just as a human person, who may or may not appeal to me. I always start like that, but then the change. I know who I am, so I know and see who he is. He is *Christ* to me, even in his human form. More than that, we all have mannerisms, habits, ways of saying and doing things in which we are different from each other, and this can rub each other the wrong way. But since I know that I am as God *means* me to be, warts and all, so I know my brother is as God means *him* to be, and we love and accept each other as we are, for we are Christ to each other.

And when clay feet appear in us (and they do), in habits that we have which at least *appear* as flesh turning up, we still say that is how God means my brother at present to be. *He* will be taking care of any changes that are needed. We are all being "conformed to the image of His Son." My part is to have it fixed in my faith that God *is doing* that in my brother, as I see Christ perfect in him. That saves me from being judgmental of him. The time may come when the Lord gives me the freedom to talk things over with him. This is where what Jesus said about the mote and beam takes effect. If I have the beam in my eye, it means that I am seeing my brother's weak spot more vividly than enjoying Christ in him. I cannot then take out his mote. But if my love and esteem of my brother is greater than any lesser shortcomings, and he senses that, then he is likely to hear me about his mote. So this is the beautiful way in which our brother is always Christ to us in his human form; and whenever he is less than that to me and the clay feet are obsessing me, *I* am the one off-center more than he. I adjust myself to who *I am*, and I have nothing then which obscures my clear sight of him as who *he is*. Always the single eye to my brother, as to Christ.

Chapter Forty-three

Body Healing

Faith also influences my attitude toward my physical health. Our bodies, especially when sick, are very real to us. We cannot help being body-minded. The immense appeal of any healing ministry, naturally, is the hope of a body healing; and we know that as in the days of Jesus there were wonderful healings, so also there are today. Some people have and use the healing gifts which Paul mentioned among the gifts of the Spirit.

But Paul did plainly warn us all that our bodies are not to be redeemed until the resurrection. "We ourselves groan within ourselves, waiting for the adoption, to wit, the redemption of our body" (Rom. 8:23). Only about our bodies did he say that we are saved in hope, and "hope that is seen is not hope" (vs. 24). In everything else we walk by faith and may experience immediate deliverances. But our outer man perishes, and the majority of us have body infirmities of some kind, whether eyes, teeth, ears or elsewhere. So we can easily be very body-minded. But I find the answer to this in the fact that I am not a body person, but a spirit person tabernacled in my body. Therefore, whatever my body condition, I keep reminding myself that I am in God's eternal life, and in perfect spirit health, and that's the real health.

Then when I have some attack of sickness, I first accept it as from God, for all is always from Him, and therefore He means me to be like that for the moment. I do not put a desire for physical healing first, but I see myself in Christ's eternal health . . . and praise Him, though that's not easy when in pain.

But then I can also rely on Paul's words in Romans 8:11, that the Spirit of Him who raised up Jesus from the dead dwells in me and "shall . . . quicken our mortal bodies"; and I can enlarge that from "shall quicken" to "does quicken," for He does dwell in us. So I take body quickening for granted, and look also for healing. I take what medical remedies are available, but I am inwardly maintaining my position of being in God's health. As we do this—I along with many others—we have proved both the quickenings and body healings. Yet not always. There are those who are *not* healed, and though they long for it—and may be experiencing questionings and travail—they accept their condition as from God. Usually they have to fight the battle of faith in refusing condemnation from those who say that they lack faith or they would be healed. That is good for them, because it gives them experience in not taking questionings about their faith from man; for they learn to have the inner peace which comes only as we hear *God's* voice, and that gives light and assurance. Then Christ is very specially magnified in them, as they still praise Him and adjust their lives to ministering His love to others.

When requests for prayer are asked for in a meeting, the majority given are for people in their sick condition in the hospital and so on. It would be good if such requests were channeled into prayers that the sick ones should be praising the Lord in their sickness, so that those around them might see the victory of faith. Then the prayers for the physical healing would only be secondary, and that is proper.

Chapter Forty-four

From Spirit Action to Body Action

We have now seen how the Holy Spirit flows out of us in rivers on our fatherhood, or ascension, or royal priesthood level—Spirit through our spirit, by the launches of faith unlimited. Being on such a level means advancing from faith as the almost subconscious background of our life in Christ—and that is marvelous in itself—to faith consciously recognized and continuously used as the "Open sesame," the Aladdin's lamp, to God's unlimited treasure chamber. Not an incident or condition of life is outside its reach: "All things are possible to him that believeth." The word of faith may be applied to even the commonest daily incidents, such as the loss of a pin or the loss of a job, or to the salvation of the unsaved and the changing of a community. It is applicable not just to so-called religious activity, but extends to all of life, for we now know there's really no difference between the secular and the spiritual.

Once the Spirit has revealed faith to us as the principle of achievement in all life, the key to the handling of all evil as well as good, we can say that life is never less than "the adventure of adversity" (as I called it in that little book *Touching the Invisible*).

And it is. I would not be writing this if it were not so. But again I say it is conditioned on this third-level understanding of *the word of faith* as the weapon of our warfare by which we "fight the good fight of faith," and not works. From our new position in the heavenlies we are not being handled by life, but rather are handling it.

So we now move on to the other channel through which the river of the Spirit is flowing—our bodies. Here again there is what I would call the normal level of His working and the revealed "special level." The normal level is that from the moment the Holy Spirit takes possession of our bodies at the new birth, both as His temple and lighthouse, we cannot help ourselves. We are under a new drive! My body formerly was used for fleshly self-satisfaction; now it is for benefiting others. As one has just written me: "I'm learning the times I am fulfilled are when the Lord is using me for others."

Precisely. The God of *other-love* has taken us over at our new birth. There is that something in us which gives us no rest until we share with others this priceless treasure which is now ours. We can't help it. Knowing we once were on the road to eternal death, but now have eternal life!—we have to tell others. We cannot but speak of the things we have seen and heard. When Christ became real to me at the age of eighteen I was not yet a vigorous witness, but I had to write of it to my mother from my English boarding school, Marlborough College; and I had to tell my closest friend at school (now a bishop) what had happened to me. In those days, at our English "public schools," it was a rare thing to find a master or boy who had any living experience of Christ, and indeed when I told my friend what had happened, he commented, "If that is Christianity, none of *us* have it!"

So I'm saying the "normal" is that by some means or another we are witnesses. As Jesus said, men don't light a lamp and put it under a bushel but on a lampstand, so that it lights the whole house. The Spirit in us compels us to be His witnesses by one means or another. Our bodies are used by Him so that by work or word, Jesus is reaching others.

Our witness is intensified as the Spirit is consciously given full control of our bodies. In my own young life, a few months after my new birth, His uncomfortable challenge came to me through a small booklet to break the one close friendship I had with a girl who did not want to go all the way for Jesus, but just remain "a good church girl." I knew God had spoken, and I wriggled this way and that for weeks. But the Spirit kept saying to me, "You can't have Christ and anti-Christ in your heart." The final break cost me plenty at the moment of doing it; but with my body-interests now freed from a lesser attraction, the Spirit at once took right over. I had just received my commission and was joining my regiment as a soldier in World War I; and it simply grabbed me that I must get eternal life to my fellow soldiers, officers and men . . . as we would soon be facing death in the trenches, for we all joked about becoming "cannon fodder." My colonel did not like my effort and I lost promotion by it, but I did witness.

So there are varying degrees of intensity in the Spirit's use of our bodies to bring Christ to others, progressing from our new birth to our conscious body-commitment to Christ. Indeed, we cannot be born again by the Spirit of other-love and not have our first urgings to share Christ with others—and this is really the beginning of the fatherhood level, for in actual fact, all levels are already in us in Christ.

Chapter Forty-five

On to Intercession

Now when we come consciously into this third level, the Spirit all the more consumes us with the desire to bring others to the liberation which is now ours—not only in the new birth, but in the fullness of the Spirit-filled life, with Christ in us as us. Not one of us can be in this union life without this desire being—even if manifested in a hundred different ways—the only basic aim we have. We are bondslaves. The zeal of God's house eats us up. Our love of Christ, as Jesus said to Peter, takes the ceaseless form (as God brings folks to us or we go to them) of feeding His lambs and feeding His sheep. We become a fiddle with one string. Christ is our main topic of conversation. In place of sharing the scandals of life, we are thrilled to share what we see of Christ leading captivity captive. We are scandal-mongers of a different type!

But just as in our inner faith-activities—in the outflowing of the Spirit through our *spirit*—we move on from the normal faith-level of all God's redeemed people to the total use of faith in the management of all life, so now in the Spirit's use of our *body*.

This body use we speak of by the Bible word "intercessor." Nothing can be tied down to a word, but "intercessor" does conveniently explain what the Bible tells us of the Spirit's action through our body. It is really the Spirit making full use of His body temples, precisely as He did of the human body temple of God's own Son, who "through the eternal Spirit offered Himself without spot unto God." We see that the final glory of being a person is the saving of others at the price of ourself. It is as with Jesus: "He saved others; Himself He cannot save" was how they mocked Him as He hung on that cross.

So we are now reaching the final and highest point in God's world-purposes through His family of sons—those who respond to His call to be intercessors. This is Paul's "pressing toward the mark for the prize of the *high calling* of God in Christ Jesus."

The body is the localized individual means by which the Spirit reaches out through us. By our human spirits He can reach out universally and can encompass everything—by faith unlimited. By our bodies He can do only one specific thing, and a different one by each particular body. So this is His highest personalized activity for us, and the highest for each of us. It was said by Jesus, "A body hast Thou prepared Me"; and by this one special body-commitment the Son said to the Father, "Lo, I come to do Thy will, O God." In this world of body people it was only by His body that "we are sanctified by the offering of the body of Jesus once for all." By that one offering "He has perfected for ever them that are sanctified" (Heb. 10:5, 7, 14).

Therefore it is *only by our bodies* that God can fulfill His saving purpose in this body world. Let us have this plainly understood. Our service to Christ is only fulfilled by some body action of ours—by body dedication. Only by this means does redemption reach the multimillion bodies of our human brotherhood. There still is for us a body death and body involvement by which God's saving purposes are fulfilled, as by His own Son's body. This is intercession.

This is a far cry from the loose way in which we Christians continually talk of intercession in terms of intercessory prayer. Intercession is the whole mountain of which prayer is one peak. There are only one or two places in Scripture where the word intercession is linked just to prayer. So let us lift it out and put it in its full perspective, and see that we ourselves accept our highest privilege as intercessors, who are also saying "A body hast Thou prepared me . . . . Lo, I come to do Thy will, O God"; and each in his unique calling into intercession.

Intercession is revealed in the Bible as God looking for special men by whom He will give some special deliverance. In Isaiah 59:16, God wonders that there is no man, no intercessor, among Israel in its backslidden condition; and then the prophet leaps on from Israel's failure to have the-man-for-that-moment to speak of the-Man-for-the-whole-of-history: "And the Redeemer shall come to Zion . . . [for] My Spirit is upon thee" (59:20–21).

So we see the intercessor is the Spirit Himself through His chosen bodies. And the way of intercession is "death" in the soul and body of the human intercessor that others might live. Of Jesus it was said: "He hath poured out His soul unto death . . . and He bare the sin of many, and made intercession for the transgressors" (Isa. 53:12).

And that means a completed task. "It is finished"; and when finished, the intercession is gained and the fruit of it appears. It was said of the ascended Jesus, "Wherefore He is able to save them to the uttermost that come unto God by Him, seeing He ever liveth to make intercession for them" (Heb. 7:25). That was the completed intercession of the great High Priest.

So it is the calling still today of us as priest-intercessors to fill up that which is behind of the afflictions of Christ for His body's sake. It is the law of harvest: "Except a corn of wheat fall into the ground and die, it abideth alone; but if it die, it bringeth forth much fruit." If a corn of wheat remains comfortably in its bin, it feeds no one. If it is sown into the ground, wrought upon by rain, snow, and frost, it disintegrates, but reappears as food for the world. That is the general body principle of intercession, just as we saw a general spirit principle of faith.

Chapter Forty-six

What is an Intercessor?

Now let us examine it more closely. We would again say it for those within hearing distance: There is suffering as well as glory in this. We all come to the cross for salvation, then we take our place on the cross for our union, and we now can take up our individual cross for the world, if we are willing to. The first two are necessities, the third is voluntary. "Take it up, if you wish," and this time for others.

The first form intercession takes is *commission*. The Spirit causes me to know that there is something He will do, and do it by me, specifically. It is not something I sought, but it sought me. I'm simply caught by it and cannot escape. I just find myself immersed in it and obsessed by it. So get this clear: It is not a matter of my running around and trying to *find* my commission. No, *it finds me. It is from the Holy Spirit*. Don't try and find such a commission. That will be the old snare of self-effort. If not conscious of such a specific commission, then I can say to the Lord who is living His life by me, "If You give me such a commission, You'll make me know it. If not, I just tell You I am ready."

Such a commission is no passing thing. It is not a

prayer I can take up and put down. It is not participating in various interests and activities. It is *"This one thing I do."* It will be the main drive of my life until it is gained.

Then when conscious of the commission, I respond like Isaiah, "Here am I; send me." By that I mean my body is wholly available, which of course includes my soul with its emotions, and my concentrated thought-processes. And somewhere along that line is coming travail and death. There will be *a price paid* equivalent to a death; but there again, we do not seek that out or make it up. He brings us into it and through it. We may not even recognize the death process until we are well into it. It may mean literal sacrifice of all that goes with our body living: our time, our faculties, our possessions, our finances, our homes, and usually most costly and common of all, our reputation. Misunderstanding and even opposition may arise in our own family circle, among our friends, our social circle, our church fellowship, or right out to the public. As we go through or have gone through our intercession, we shall well know where we have died.

One who brought to light the principle of intercession to the church in our generation was Rees Howells, to whom I have several times referred. He always spoke concerning intercession as "the firstfruits going to the altar," which referred in type to the meal offering of Leviticus 2. There the first handful of the flour is burned on the altar, and the rest feeds the priests. By that he meant that there would be this "death" in which the self-life, the body-soul life, has had its human setbacks, sacrifice, maybe failure in the eyes of the world or church, and out of that death came the life to others. It is the 2 Corinthians 4:7–12 principle, but this time in specific rather than general form—for this is where Paul is speaking about bearing in our body the dying of the Lord Jesus. He then writes, "So death worketh in us, but life in you."

The intercession is completed, first by being gained on the level of faith, as the intercessor becomes settled in his inner consciousness that the Lord has done it; and second, by his own continued involvement in it, by whatever action accompanies it, while the Spirit brings the thing to pass. And it continues until the intercessor knows that his part in it is *fulfilled*.

Commission. Cost. Completion.

Chapter Forty-seven

An Example: Personal

Here are a few personal instances. When at Cambridge after World War I, I was unable to take part in my favorite games of "rugger" and field hockey because of a wounded leg. But I had one overwhelming urge—to get around to all the rooms of the men in my College, Trinity, and witness to them and ask them to join our then-small group of the Cambridge InterCollegiate Christian Union, commonly called C.I.C.C.U. I did this, though often it cost me a lot to do it, for they were mainly men who had held good ranks in the army and were pretty sophisticated, being older than the average undergraduates. Then, with only two terms left to complete my degree, the call of God came clear to me to leave the University and join C.T. Studd and his small band, who had been alone in the heart of Africa all the war years. I did not do this easily, because it was against the advice of my friends, and according to Cambridge rules I could not return later and pick up where I dropped out. But I did do it, and it was "death" to me on that level.

But before I left, near the end of that term, the Spirit distinctly came on me to go and speak in no uncertain terms to all I knew personally who had not accepted Christ, or who at least showed no sign of spiritual life—men whom I never expected to see again in this life. I went and pulled no punches, and a number came out for Christ, about sixteen of them. This caused a stir like a touch of revival and the C.I.C.C.U. men asked me to come and tell them about it. As I did so, it came like a vision to me that every university and college in Britain and the world should have its evangelical and witnessing union, as we had. So I suggested to two of my friends that we take a hall in London and invite some from Oxford and London and other colleges, and hold an intervarsity conference. About sixty of us attended. Little did I then realize that this was the start of what has since grown to become the world-wide InterVarsity Fellowship, now in hundreds and probably thousands of colleges in all nations, developed under the dedicated leadership of Douglas Johnson and Oliver Barclay in Britain, Howard Guinness in Canada and Australia, and Stacey Woods in the U.S.A. and on through the world. There had been this definite "commission" that I *had* to give myself to witness in the university. There had also been an unexpected form of "death"—in not remaining to get my degree, though it entailed only a couple of terms. But the intercession was gained on this far larger scale, as the IVF has become this world-wide student fellowship.

Again, after Pauline and I returned to England in 1931 to carry on the home end, God's commission to our Worldwide Evangelization Crusade was to go to any unevangelized area of the world. It was our custom then for those at the home end to take a slightly larger share of what monthly money there was before it was apportioned to the fields, as it cost more to live in England than in Africa. But when we had practically nothing to send to the thirty-five missionaries (I have already told how we were nearly penniless that first month), the Lord clearly said to Pauline and me, "Why not personally live by the injunction to 'take no thought for food and clothing... but seek first the kingdom of God and His righteousness,' and believe the promise that 'all these things will be added unto you'?"

We saw the point and accepted it from God, though to us at that time it was a big thing—having no earthly source of supply, not even from the mission—and we also thought at that time we should never get anyone else to join us in the work of the home end on those same conditions! But how way off we were, for our WEC co-workers (maybe over a hundred of them at all our home bases round the world) all these years have taken no mission funds for personal needs, but have lived by the promises of God.

In those first days we did sometimes touch bottom. When we were about a dozen of us, we lived for a week in our London home with no household supplies. At mealtimes we joined in the fellowship room, intending to thank the Lord for the bread of life! But the retired lady's maid of C.T. Studd's mother lived with us in our basement, where we also had our kitchen and dining room. Though she did not outwardly profess Christ she really loved our young men, whom she called "Hallelujah Boys"—and all we knew was that each day at mealtime the bell rang from downstairs. We trooped down to find bread, cheese and tea on the table. We always thanked the Lord that, having asked only for daily bread, we got cheese on top! We could only guess that Miss Mussett put it there. Also, for months we lived practically entirely on sacks of lentils sent us by a Christian farmer . . . but that was Daniel's food, and we flourished on it. Sometimes, though, we felt like the children of Israel who cried to God for quails and then got them until they "came out of their nostrils"! But those were early days and it has rarely happened since.

It seemed to us more an adventure of faith than a death to ourselves; yet it was a spark which set us alight in our divine commission. The commission was on us to see that all those unevangelized areas of the world which were brought to our attention were entered and occupied, God sending the stream of recruits to enter them. What exploits of faith there were in the entry of some of them! But this is not the place for those stories. Year by year we did that, opening a new field every year, until we are now on forty fields. And we have already mentioned how the gospel has been going out to tens of thousands, and how living churches have been founded which are now continuing with their own witness in many lands of Africa . . . and in Indonesia, India, Thailand, Japan, South America, Europe, and elsewhere. Pauline and I had that specific commission; we knew we had it, and that it must be fulfilled. God told us to take this way of personal *financial* death, which has become our home-base principle ever since. The intercession has been fulfilled—our part in it—by the establishment of these many fields in many countries. We meanwhile gained our individual intercession by it becoming easy for us, ever since, to trust the Lord for personal finances and to take our share in the stand of faith for the increasingly large finances needed by the Crusade throughout the world—with no appeals made to man.

I would say that, right up to today, God gives us the privilege of being intercessors. As my years in our direct WEC activities ceased, the Lord gave me the plain calling—another definite commission—to get around the U.S.A. with the message of union and replacement in Christ which has been the mainstream of this book. I had to do it. I had to go round and repeat unendingly what God has made so real to me. There are always new facets of light, but the heart of the message is ever the same. The price of this intercession is to continue nonstop into my eighties, even though my old leg injury makes walking a difficulty—though in fact, you don't notice the dying when absorbed in the harvesting. And now, after going round for about ten years, the Lord Himself has called in co-intercessors, all unknown to me. Bill and Marge Volkman had the call from God five years ago to start the *Union Life Magazine,* which is now spreading widely and being the voice of the Spirit to many. Dan and Barbara Stone and Jan Ord have also had the call of God to give themselves full-time to the spread of the message—all looking to the Lord alone for their material supplies. Bill and Anne Mortham take charge of our summer fellowship center in Wisconsin, a gift from Bill Volkman to us all. But the real heartbeat of our fellowship comes from the families who open their homes and sponsor gatherings for us all around the U.S.A. and Canada, besides about a hundred others who are listed as Union Life contacts in the various states. A first footing has been established in Britain also, with Janet Inger, Frances Heys, and Fred and Amy Dagnell being full-time with us. Not that we are some exclusive group, but are one in Christ with all who give the full message of the gospel—seeking to make our own contribution, as given us by God, to "the perfecting of the saints unto the work of the ministry and the edifying of the body of Christ." For Pauline and me an intercession has been gained, and the harvest is being widely reaped.

Chapter Forty-eight

Examples: Two Men of God

I am reluctant to use personal illustrations like the foregoing when there are so many around me, among my Crusade and Union Life fellow workers, who could fill books with like experiences. However, I can give these personal ones in more detail. And it is always my faith that others of you who read this will catch the revelation from the Spirit and the Scriptures that the call to and privilege of being an intercessor is *something special*. It is obviously available to us all who in Christ are royal priests; but it requires Commission, Cost, Completion—consciously entered into and then gained. A person may even look back on his life and detect, as I can, where he was being an intercessor and yet did not know that was what he was—but now see that it was the law of the harvest being fulfilled. However, because I now know what it is to be an intercessor with the Spirit Intercessor in me, I can more effectively gain an intercession and help others to their "high calling."

The most outstanding examples of intercession—and ones which greatly influenced me—are the lives of C.T. Studd and Rees Howells.

C.T. STUDD

C.T. Studd left for the heart of Africa in 1913, leaving behind his wife, apparently a permanent invalid with an enlarged heart, who was spending half her days in bed. He had to go, he said, and it was the only time he went against the wishes even of his own wife; and when a friend came to tell him that it was not even Christian to leave her in that condition, he wrote on a postcard what became the motto of the Crusade: "If Jesus Christ be God and died for me, then no sacrifice can be too great for me to make for Him."

He went. He found his "black gold" in the Ituri Forest of the Congo. But before reaching there, he wrote back to tell his wife of how he had nearly died on safari of a severe attack of fever. He had one young man with him, Alfred Buxton, and when thinking that he would not be alive by the next morning, he called Alfred into his tent to tell him so. But as Alfred left the tent, "C.T." remembered the promise in James that those who call, when they're ill, for the elders of the church and are anointed in the name of the Lord, will be healed. So he called Alfred back—Alfred being twenty years old—and said to him, "Alfred, I hereby appoint you an elder of the church of Jesus Christ!" Then he said to him, "Get some oil. All we have is in the kerosene lamp—but the scripture isn't particular—so get some and anoint me." He did so and the fever was gone by the next day. So he then in his letter to his wife said, "Scilla, don't trust those earthly doctors. Trust Doctor Jesus and get off your bed." This she did, and began to go through England and the U.S.A. with a fiery challenge to young men and women, of whom I was one, to go and join her husband in getting the gospel to those tribes. So involved were these two at the two ends of the young mission that in the last sixteen years of their lives they saw each other *only for one short visit of two weeks!* That was a long-drawn-out "death." I know what it cost her—in a way, much more than him—as she was my mother-in-law. She remained "at home" while he was immersed in all the absorbing and dangerous activities of his pioneer life. But note: You don't choose your own "death" in your intercession; God puts it on you as you proceed. "Our light affliction, which is but for a moment, worketh for us a far more exceeding and eternal weight of glory."

But the price was fully paid, the intercession gained, both in the heart of Africa and in the world-wide extensions of the Crusade to which I have already referred. The full story, which has had tens of thousands of fascinated readers and has resulted in many being called into full-time service for the Lord, has been written in his biography, which is now available in a number of languages.* Once again, this illustrates the three principles of intercession—Commission, Cost, and Completion.

REES HOWELLS

The life story of Rees Howells must be read, as it is by many thousands these days, to catch the continual stream of instances of how the Holy Spirit first got His total possession of that young life, and

---

*C. T. Studd, Cricketer and Pioneer, published by Lutterworth Press in Britain and distributed by the Christian Literature Crusade in the U.S.A.

Examples: Two Men of God

then began to give him early practice in specific intercessions. There was the derelict of a man living in the boiler room of the tin mill; the tramps; the unemployed villagers; the sick people; and the succession of deliverances having to do with buying the four large properties for the Bible College and School. Each has a fascinating story of "deaths" which led into the gaining of them. Finally he lost his reputation—and perhaps never regained it. For he had a word from the Lord, together with his co-intercessors at the College, just before the start of World War II, that for the next thirty years the world would be kept open for the gospel and a thousand more missionaries would go out from the College. He called it the Thirty Years Vision.

Then came Hitler and Mussolini and the outbreak of the war, with the threat that these two men would take over the world and close it to all missionary witness. Rees Howells first countered that by publishing a book called *God Challenges the Dictators,* which openly declared that God would destroy these men who were clamping down on the spread of the gospel. Rees Howells would have been one of the first men to be liquidated if Hitler had conquered Britain!

He then went further. He announced, by the word of the Lord, the day the war would be ended. There had been that first year of so-called war when nothing happened, and we joked about it as "The Phony War"—the French just sitting cozily behind their Maginot line. It was at the end of that year that he called for the celebration of victory to be on Whitsunday of 1941. Some of the national newspapers took up the "prophecy." But that was the very week when the *real war broke out*, not ended, with the shock of Hitler's Panzer invasion of Holland, Belgium and France—and threatening Britain. If ever there was a false prophet! His reputation was lost forever. But he held to his Whitsunday celebration. He had gained the victory and the destruction of the dictators *by faith*, and there he stood.

It actually took four years before the victory was a visible fact. Surely a crazy and mistaken faith. It may have looked like that then, but not now. We couldn't then see that Hitler had built up such an enormous armament that unless it was wholly destroyed, even if there should be a so-called peace, the free world would have lived faced with a constant threat. In those four years that threat disappeared forever, with the entry of the U.S.A. into the war, and the final destruction of the Nazi and Japanese power.

During those years Rees Howells and his co-intercessors at the College stood on their faith ground. They confronted the challenge of Rommel on the verge of the capture of Alexandria, which would have opened the door for an invasion of the Holy Land, and they got through to the victory of faith which declared that he would *never* capture Alexandria—and they made that word of faith known. No one had then heard or thought of Montgomery and the way in which he turned Rommel and his army back in flight.

It was the same when the German army had invaded Russia and reached Stalingrad. If they had taken that city, they could have crossed the Caucasus and invaded the Holy Land by that route. The College stood their ground in faith that the Nazis would never take that city. The battle raged for weeks, and the surrender of the German army there was the beginning of the end of the German invasion of Russia.

Then, with the war ended, there came the real gain of this intercession, far beyond anticipation—as Paul puts it, "exceeding abundantly above all that we ask or think." With all opposition ended, and the dictators destroyed just as Rees Howells by the word of faith had said they would be, a tremendous upsurge of the gospel throughout the world began. We who are involved in missions know there has been nothing like it in world history. There have been hundreds of new missionary recruits, at more than double the rate before the war, and all kinds of new missionary agencies. But far more important, the freedom of the world from colonial governments has meant many nations finding their identity. Their churches and believers, the fruit of a century and more of missionary labors, have begun to rise up. They have claimed their inheritance as autonomous churches of Jesus Christ with His Word and Spirit and have begun to take their place of leadership both in the spread of the gospel among their own people and in sending their own missionaries to other lands. There is a wholly new "bursting at the seams" of the church of Christ in whole continents like Africa and South America, and in many countries such as Indonesia, Korea, and elsewhere in the Far East.

So we see that the gaining of the intercession for which God called Rees Howells and those with him to lay their lives on the altar, accompanied by "the first fruits going to the altar" (Lev. 2:1–3) in that loss of reputation, has in God's perfect timetable produced this unbelievable world harvest, beyond what any of us fifty years ago would have dreamed of; and this could not have been produced without the time it took for the destruction of the Nazi menace and the freedom of the years that have followed. It was an intercession gloriously gained, but only seen by those whose eyes are opened to the law of intercession: the corn-of-wheat principle—through death to life. This is what Rees Howells used to make so plain in his teaching on the lives of the Bible intercessors—from Noah, Abraham, Moses, Isaiah, Jonah, Daniel, right through to the Savior Himself, and on to Paul and up to our day. Samuel, Rees Howells' son, has cooperated with Doris Ruscoe in preparing a further book on some of those teachings.*

**Intercession: Readings from Rees Howells,* published in the U.S.A. by Christian Literature Crusade and distributed in Britain by Lutterworth Press.

Chapter Forty-nine

An Intercessor in Marriage

I want to delve a bit more deeply, by way of illustration, into a "more personal" area of intercession, where it touches on the use of our affections.

There is a close friend of mine among the many with whom we are linked in fellowship. She knows who she is: Christ in her human form. Her husband was in a good professional position and a good home-provider, but he showed no outward response to Christianity. The time came when she discovered, as a great shock, that he was having an ongoing adulterous relationship with a married woman. She faced out with the Lord the shock, hurt and resentment. What should she do? Knowing that she was not herself but Christ in her, she knew the difference between her soul hates and resentments and the love she had for her husband in her spirit, for it was God loving him by her; and just as important, she recognized that God *meant* her husband to be tangled up in his sex life to expose his own need to him. So instead of a marital blowout and possible divorce, she informed her husband that she had found out what was going on, but that she loved him as ever—for he was her husband and she his wife.

That shook him! When he expected a blast, he got only a confirmation of her unchanged love. This brought a reply to her which was another shock—a good one. He said, "Well, if that is Christianity, I can listen to it!"

The result was that after some weeks, while she knew the adulterous relationship continued, the moment came when she told her husband that she would like to meet with him and the woman. They agreed. The three met—and surely this would be the time for strong words by my friend. Instead, she just accepted facts as facts (despite her inner hurt) and said to them, "It can't go on like this. Make the choice. Either go with her and leave me and the children, or break off the relationship and return to me." The husband and the woman both agreed. The severance was made, and he returned home. But far more than that, God has done such a transforming work in him, with repentance and renewal, that he is now a strong witness for Christ and busy helping other men who get caught in that same trap.

This is intercession. With little said about the inner-death way in which she walked—which was the background for her steadfast love, and at the right moment, holy boldness—she gained the intercession by the Spirit Intercessor in her, doubtless with "groanings that cannot be uttered."

Another close friend had an experience somewhat the same. Her husband holds a public position in his profession and is a man who loves the Lord. What a shock when she found out that he had a secret liaison, with visits to a motel, with one who was a close friend in whom she confided.

She first challenged her husband about this

adultery over the phone. He is an honest man who knows the Lord, and he admitted his descent into the flesh, and his sin against God and wrong against her. But then he added, "If the woman's husband learns of this, he is a man of such influence that he could destroy me in my profession." My friend's answer straightaway to her unfaithful husband was, "I am your wife. If you have a crash professionally, then I crash along with you."

The result of that was that the husband—who, as I say, knows the Lord—took one big jump of faith right then and there, and he has told me how he moved from being the struggling and defeated man of Romans 7 to the liberated man in Romans 8. He saw "in a flash of the Spirit" that there was no more condemnation, and that he was released "by the law of the Spirit of life in Christ Jesus." The result in their marriage is that where there had been an unhappy relationship between them, it has so changed that she now tells me her husband is her best friend!

As for the woman who had so wronged and deceived her, the day my friend first heard of this she called the florist and ordered one white rose in a vase to be sent to her. There was admission of guilt, but it took time for a real heart repentance. But the day came when she plainly told my friend that she had not before *really* admitted her wrongdoing, and she asked for forgiveness. My friend's answer: "I need forgiveness just as much from you, because of my hate and resentful attitude towards you." And there was a time of reconciliation.

Chapter Fifty

True Love and Infatuation

Another form of intercession is also on a deeply personal level and may well be misunderstood by those who have not learned the right use of their soul-body outer affections.

To start with, as we have intimated when looking into spirit-soul relationships (see Chapter 30): Do any of us know and become settled in the difference between soul-affection and spirit-love without some death-and-resurrection experience of it? The strongest form of desire is misguided soul-body "inordinate affection," which we can mistake for love. It is Paul who calls it "inordinate affection" (Col. 3:5), the misuse of the flesh in its "affections and lusts," which he says we have crucified (Gal. 5:24); and "flesh" is only another word for soul-body.

Human flesh is God's precious way of manifesting Himself. Jesus was "God manifested in the flesh." "Sinful flesh" resulted from Satan capturing our flesh through its "affections and lusts"—flesh misused for self-gratification. But our Christ in His death "condemned sin in the flesh" (Rom. 8:3), threw sin out of ownership and put it behind bars. This means that sin no longer owns the flesh but is a condemned criminal behind bars, awaiting execution. Meanwhile, however, it shouts at us from behind its bars by using temptations of the flesh. One of these is the use of our soul-body emotions and affections for self-gratification in some diversionary "love"—as if it were genuine love—which is what Paul calls "inordinate affection" and what we here call *infatuation*.

But God's love, self-giving love, which is now ours, is other-love. It may or may not be manifested through our soul-emotion and body-desire; but should it be, the emotion is *not* the love but only an outer expression of it. God's love, our love as He, is a laying of ourself on the altar for others: spirit-love, a will-love, even when without the emotions of soul-love.

This is supremely so in marriage when the chemistry of the soul-body attractions has simmered down or gone into the background. Love is then the two living together, as one of my friends writes, "when we are for each other, keeping each other where we belong in Christ. It is the reality of a loving God who is living in us for each other."

Indeed, husband and wife then never raise the question of whether they love each other. Of course they do, for love means that each has given himself for the other in their marriage bond "till death do us part." That love is expressed in the practical self-giving of both in all aspects of their family life; and when both are the Lord's, in the additional bond of spiritual fellowship and service. That is *the* love, of which physical and emotional love is a beautiful ingredient, but by no means the central reality of the love-bond.

But to go still further, the deepest revelation and

understanding of true marriage is that all we who are in Christ are inwardly—each of us in our own self—married to Christ; so we are each inwardly bride to Bridegroom, wife to Husband. That is the only eternal and real marriage, and thus all God's redeemed people have an inward *marriage of the Spirit.*

Our outer physical marriage is really a symbol of this eternal inner marriage; and that is why marriage is one to one, is not to be violated by an illicit union, and is not to be destroyed by divorce. This is what Paul is saying in Ephesians 5:25–33: "For this cause shall a man leave his father and mother, and shall be joined unto his wife, and they two shall be one flesh. This is a great mystery; but I speak concerning Christ and the church" (vss. 31–32).

As a result, when we do understand and recognize our true, eternal marriage, we do not overrate our earthly marriage, or mistake it as our true marriage. It is only as shadow to substance, symbol to reality; and we see our earthly marriage as a means of exemplifying the true, eternal union.

Many of us don't know this ultimate truth about marriage, and so I repeat it. Each of us has our true Husband within us, we being the bride of Christ. That is the only eternal and true marriage union. Our flesh marriage is an earthly figure of it, by which we learn its joys and responsibilities, and is meant to be secondary to our true marriage. If we mistake our earthly marriage for the real one, we soon find that its hold on us weakens as the dominant factor in our lives, because it is not! It is, certainly, a fixed earthly union, but is only the shadow of the substance. For us who know this, a divorce cannot be considered or be in our vocabulary. "Let it not be named among you, as becometh saints" (Eph. 5:13).

But until we have learned to recognize the difference between spirit and soul love, it is extremely common for us to have a sudden soul-body attraction for one who is not our mate—and this can be devastatingly strong, for God created us with strong soul and body affections for His use. Then, if we have not learned our lesson, this sudden infatuation can fill us with guilt and condemnation. If we do not yet know or are unsettled in the truth that our soul and body as well as our spirit are wholly God's, and in His total control and keeping, we can remain in great turmoil and suffer distressing temptation—or even be swept off our feet into sin—and we may appear to ourselves to be unfaithful to our mate when we are not. (Of course, those who have not been born of the Spirit can know *only* flesh love, and divorces these days are the common way of exchanging one flesh love for another.)

Even those of us who are God's people may—if we have not yet grasped this division between soul and spirit—easily confuse the attraction of a soul-body "inordinate affection" with true, inner, spirit-love. It diverts us like a rival and adulterous "love." And should our mate also not recognize the difference between infatuation and real love, he or she may be consumed with jealousy or retaliation. Let us not mistake the temporary invasion of a soul-affection for the permanent reality of the spirit-love which has bound us in marriage.

Many of us, including myself, have had such an invasion of soul-love, both being condemned by it and intensely resisting it. But by that means we have learned a great secret—that the response to a soul-affection is not to resist or condemn it, but to recognize it for what it is and then use it for another purpose. We use it, and indeed swallow it up, by turning it into an opportunity to express *God's love* towards that one who has attracted us. That means I inwardly "fight the battle through" by setting my affections in only *one direction*, with only *one purpose and desire*: that the one who has attracted me will have Christ fully formed in her or him—as in me. That is the single eye of faith and so the soul-affection becomes a channel of spirit other-love.

And—though it may take time when the soul-affection is strong—the whole condition is reversed from guilt and condemnation over the temptation into being a means of intercession for the other: that by my dying to a misuse of soul-affection there is a rising—first in me, by which I gain the intercession, and then in the other one—of the reality of Christ within. I have proved that as fact, for it happened just like that, as the intercession was walked and gained.

If one becomes aware of such a soul-affection in his or her mate, and at first is disturbed or jealous because of it, if he (say it is a man), rather, by faith-knowing will believe that his mate is really still fixedly bound in spirit-love to *him*, and will hold steady—having faith (that is, his intercession) that his mate will use that outer soul-affection for the forming of Christ in the other individual—then there will be no question raised about her continued fixedness in her mated love for him.

I know one close friend, a husband, who loves the Lord. His wife was caught by such an enslaving affection toward another man. But God used that to show her *once for all* the difference between soul-love and spirit-love, and settled her back in her true love to her husband. Meanwhile, her husband stood steadfastly and loyally by her, though not without pain, and by this he himself grew in the Lord. They now are a wonderful couple, steady in their own family life and helping many who have like problems.

Chapter Fifty-one

A Letter of Much Insight

The fact is . . . we have long misused our souls and bodies under the old illusion that the evil was *in us,* not in Satan. We now know differently; and we know that now *Christ* is expressing Himself by us in place of Satan. Yet we, most of us, still remain suspicious of our flesh, particularly regarding sex—especially we men, most of whom have strong sex drives. We may have misused our sex in our former days. We may even have slipped since. But let us really accept that the trouble is not in our sex or flesh, but was caused by Satan (sin) in us, and that God has now replaced indwelling sin by His own total ownership of our bodies as His dwelling place. *Now* we can fully trust Him that every appetite and faculty has been put there by Him for His full, liberated use. But where we have not totally accepted that fact, we walk fearful of our body passions and think that we must keep some check or control on them—or who knows what we will do? We do not totally accept the fact that God *only* is our keeper of body and soul, as of spirit.

Paul speaks of keeping our bodies under subjection, lest we become disapproved in His service (1 Cor. 9:27). This means that we are to settle the matter that our bodies are so totally His living sacrifices that we are in total safekeeping. We cannot consider them being used for any sin purposes—and we are in full physical activity, not seeking to keep our bodies by self-effort but *by faith* and without fear.

So then, as we move right through to who we really are, *whole persons, wholly His and none other's,* we know the limits the Spirit of love has put on us. We know plainly that sex is sacred to marriage and our bodies are for our mates. So we boldly take the stand of faith—that misuse of sex is sin and is *out* for us. Paul stated it plainly: "Shall I . . . take the members of Christ and make them the members of an harlot? . . . Flee fornication. Every [other] sin . . . is outside the body; but he that committeth fornication sinneth against his own body. What? Know ye not that your body is the temple of the Holy Ghost?" (1 Cor. 6:15–20).

So this kind of sin is not in our vocabulary. Any thought in that direction is rejected. We boldly do this on the word of Scripture, inwardly confirmed to us by the Spirit, that God is our keeper as He says He is, and will keep us. We "cannot sin because [we are] born of God" (1 John 3:9). Therefore we accept our freedom in soul and body, and express our love one to another, for it is God loving by us—unafraid.

It is on this basis that some of us have used our soul-body affection—even if tempted to misuse—not to condemn ourselves, but by accepting the temptation as a door being opened for us as intercessors, for God's love to reach another.

John T. (Tony) Ketcham, a Washington lawyer, and his wife Bette, live in Bowie, Maryland, where their home is a family center for many of us who have fellowship together in the Spirit. Bette has very helpfully written to a friend on the operation of soul-affection and spirit-love, and we will all profit by it. I quote her letter at length:

> One of the big questions in my own life was always the *why* of my own apparent unfulfillment in the area of feelings! And it is a big question to be answered in each one of us who are operating now in union and thus manifesting Father's life to others. I did know, as you do too, that all that was happening in me was for others; and in the beginning, I reveled in that fact. But, as time went grinding on, my excitement of being for others began to dissipate, and my longing to feel all those "good feelings" began to choke me. It has just become a recent thing for me to know that the stress, or tension (soul-body tension), manifested in us is *necessary*; for it is the way persons in union and intercession operate.
>
> Your spirit is joined—fused—with His. That being so, the truth about you is that you can *only* be selfless and for others. Obviously your soul is not who you are (any more than light, heat, or power is electricity), but your soul has a function to perform in order for spirit to be manifested and fruit to be produced. Soul's natural appetite is to reach out and fulfill *itself*; it always will. It is of the earth, earthy, and is meant to be part of the "operating machine" we call the body. Soul doesn't run the machinery, it is only part of it. *Spirit is the operator.* As spirit in you is pure and righteous, all that comes forth from you is selfless and pure love. I believe we are to say that *pure light* is who I am, no matter how contrary the circumstances may

be, because Jesus says that we are the light of the world.

Now, if there is confusion in our minds as to just how our machinery gets in gear to produce fruit for others, we fall into false condemnation and guilt which leads to "sin." As you stated on the phone, "My soul tells me I'm selfish." If you believe that, you will live out what you believe, and sins will follow. Your spirit (married to His Spirit) is a *lover*-spirit, searching for those who are in desperate need of God's total love and acceptance. The "machinery" is put into action by your spirit when your soul is engaged by reacting and reaching out to "John Doe." You can literally feel this engagement. Something begins grinding into operation inside and we find ourselves literally reaching out for "John Doe" and loving him in every one of our senses. This is the normal and natural use of the "machinery." Part of the tension rears its head when soul realizes that the Spirit (who is "the law") will not allow a *lawless* loving. All the while, poor soul is saying "more, more," for soul's operation is to continually try to fulfill itself. Fortunately, in our union life reality, we are safe lovers. I find that I am filled with God's Spirit and I am not left to the ultimate end experienced by unfulfilled persons living on the lower level of fallen man. They must allow soul to keep running amuck, for their spirit-centers are Satanic and they must manifest the self-centered father whose lusts they are showing forth. They must constantly and continually try to fulfill themselves with no apparent end in sight. They cannot know, until the new birth in Jesus Christ, that their *only fulfillment* is in the spirit, not in the soul-body. Soul is there just to get the machinery working to react in love to others.

As intercession is brought forth and manifested through the tension of a fully operating soul and its spirit "operator," the intercessor feels the tug between the two. I quite frequently hear my spirit operator talking to the soul:

"Hold up now, soul, I'm in this unconditional love adventure of intercession for *'John Doe,'* *not* for you. I choose to draw him to Christ through your operation of reaching out to love and cherish, but I mean to meet *his* needs in your reaching, not yours. Soul, you forget so often that you are not running things; I am. You would reach and reach and then reach some more, as if that is all you are meant to do. You forget once in a while that you are not spirit, and you therefore mistakenly feel that you should be somehow 'getting' something and thus feel fulfilled. O foolish soul, the only fulfillment there is to be had is for *the spirit.* You so conveniently forget from time to time that I am a responsible and mature son in Jesus Christ, and not an irresponsible human, one whose soul does not yet have a responsible and cooperating spirit in union with God's own. Because I am in union with Christ, I cannot let you run unchecked. You will quite naturally feel as if you were still not fulfilled, but my love for 'John Doe' can only do what is best for *him.*"

Well, dearest, this is God's way in me. He has shown me that the tension of soul pulling me one way and the Spirit in me pulling the other is the operation of the "machinery." This is just how it works. I'll always be privileged to feel the pull and tug, as that is the evidence that He is in operation. Don't fear that your soul will take over, as it doesn't run anything. *Your spirit is fused with His. He'll* control your soul very nicely, thank you, as you live in the reality of your being one with Him.

Lovingly,
Bette

I think this is of sufficient importance to underline this fact again. We may have entered in by the Spirit's revelation to knowing we are He in our forms. We *know* that, as spirit joined to Spirit. But often we have not equally totally recognized that He is the owner and indweller of our *whole persons*—soul and body as much as spirit—as we read in that word of Paul's: "I pray God your whole spirit and soul and body be preserved blameless" (1 Thess. 5:23).

Therefore our soul and body are not mere appendages to be conveniently used—*they are we!* In our old misconception we wrongly thought there were evil tendencies in them, such as sex, greed, hate, jealousy, etc. Then we found out that the evil in our souls and bodies was the indwelling sin (Satan) misusing us. Then we moved on by faith recognition and inner witness to having indwelling sin replaced by indwelling Christ. But our problem is that often we're not so quick and complete in boldly recognizing that He has now taken full possession of our soul emotions and body appetites. We are *not* to walk in fear of our old excesses—as though, if we are not careful, they might recur and grab us. If we still have not had that settled in our believing, we are leaving the door open to much temptation. And we are still *partially bound,* because we live in secret fear of our soul-body rushing us into some sins. We still carry the graveclothes of some negative believing into our resurrection life. We are afraid of our temptation . . . so we must watch ourself; and we also suspiciously watch our brother and sister (or our mate) as though they still carry their graveclothes around.

So there's a further bold step needed: a total accepting of our death in Christ to *sin*, the *world*, and our *flesh* in its "affections and lusts"—recognizing it as crucified, so far as its misuses are concerned (Gal. 5:24). Against fears, suspicions, temptations, we boldly say *He* is our keeper, and He *is* doing His job and *will* do it. When any stirring strong winds of temptation blow on us, instead of fighting, or fearing, or running away, we say, "No, it is what God means us to have—the temptation that James has told us to count *all joy*." It is merely sin shouting at us through the prison bars. "But *You*, Christ," we say, "have *all* of us, including our tempted areas; and You will now *use* them to express Your self-giving love through us in place of our temptations to self-getting and self-gratification."

I think this is a further stage of total recognition of this word of Paul's earlier quoted: "And the very God of peace sanctify you wholly; and I pray God your whole spirit and soul and body be preserved blameless." The *whole* of us. So *reject* fear, for "perfect love casteth out fear." Replace it by the boldness of faith, for what you believe holds you. If we continue in the negative belief that we are so weak and temptable that we had better keep watch over ourself, then we shall have the fruits of our negative faith in temptation and bondage. If we replace these perverted believings by a bold, total, positive faith in

Him, the Total Sanctifier, we shall have the fruit of our faith, the freedom to be ourself in expression of our emotions, reasoning, and body-affections; and equally, we shall free ourself from negative suspicions and judgments of our brethren.

This will obviously appear dangerous to some who read it. And it *is*! Life in the Spirit *is* living dangerously. *Of course* it is nonsense and absurd!—not only for those still in the flesh without Christ, but also for those of us in Christ who have not yet entered into union—in death-resurrection reality—with Christ, and who therefore are fearful (as in Romans 7) of the assaults of the flesh, not knowing how to meet them. But I am writing on the third, the intercession level, where we *do know* that difference between soul and spirit, and can discern (or maybe learn by experience) that soul's inordinate affection is outer flesh-pull, not the true love of the spirit. It is of *this* I am writing—of how temptation to self-gratification can be reversed into an outgoing of the Spirit of love . . . for God's "completing work" of Christ to be formed in the object of the affections.

Chapter Fifty-two

Yes, He Is–I Am

I correspond with an Indian friend, Biva Tampoe of Madras, who read one of my books some years ago and wrote to inquire further about the life of union in Christ. Recently she sent me her only copy of a little book published by her father, the late Professor Coomarasamy Tampoe of Kavali College in Andhra Pradesh, who also taught in British universities. The book is called *The Problem of Good*. I was struck by the way he wrote of Jesus as a man who walks the same faith way as ourselves, and I am putting in my own words, at the close of this book of mine, what I found to be his stimulating outline of that faith which overcame the world, and by which, John says, we also overcome our world. I want to see *how* He walked, for John says we are to walk *as He walked*.

It is obvious from Luke's saying that Jesus "grew in wisdom and stature" that, whatever the inherent knowledge He had as to who He was, He still had to advance into an enlarged understanding of that truth. Probably Mary told Him, when old enough, of His miraculous birth, confirming to Him that He was the Son of God.

But His means of discovering the *purpose* of His

coming was from the Scriptures. We know that because, at twelve years of age, He spent three days fascinating the theologians of the temple, not by a display of any knowledge of His own, but by "hearing them and asking them questions" of a type which obviously amazed them. Then He returned to His carpenter's bench for another eighteen years. His subsequent constant reference to the Scriptures shows that this study was His main occupation those years, and from those Scriptures He saw the revelation of the coming Messiah, the anointed One of God, to found the kingdom which would have no end.

Evidently most Jewish readers of the Scriptures, and maybe even some of the prophets themselves, understood this to be as king of an earthly kingdom which would have dominion over all nations, who would pour in their wealth to Him. But there were always the men who saw in the Spirit: like Abraham, who looked for "a heavenly city"; like Moses, who said circumcision was of the heart, not flesh; like Jeremiah, who saw that all men were to have the law written in their hearts; and like Isaiah, who, full of the glory of the coming Savior, wrote of His uniqueness in being born of a virgin, His royalty as "Everlasting Father" and "Prince of peace," and His outreach extending to the Gentiles and the ends of the earth . . . but also foretold His suffering and death as our sin-bearer. From the Psalms, so full of references to Him, Jesus saw the details of His coming crucifixion, His bodily resurrection, His ascension and eternal priesthood. To those two on the road to Emmaus, after His resurrection, He "expounded in all the Scriptures, beginning at Moses and all the prophets, the things concerning Himself." Soon after that, when with His disciples, He "opened their understanding that they might understand the Scriptures" and told them: "Thus it is written, and thus it behooved Christ to suffer, and to rise from the dead the third day."

So plainly, while a carpenter at home, His eyes were fully opened to all the revelation in Scripture. But the point is that *no man can live by outer information,* not even by the account of His birth from his mother. *We can only live by fixed inner consciousness*; and so, even though Jesus was conceived of the Spirit, He had to be baptized in the Spirit to know and fulfill His life's calling. He knew His cousin John was the prophesied "voice of one crying, 'Prepare ye the way of the Lord.'" He saw the multitudes following John and repenting of their sins; and that all John could give them was that outer assurance of remission of sins. John kept telling them that Another was coming whose shoe latchet he was not worthy to unloose, and that He would give them the inner baptism of the Spirit, for by that alone could they *inwardly* know their sins were forgiven.

And what was more, though John knew (presumably from his mother) the story of his own special birth and the miracle birth of his cousin Jesus, yet he still said he did not know Him as the Messiah until His baptism. Then he and Jesus—no one else—saw the Spirit coming on Jesus in the form of a dove, and heard the voice saying to Him, "Thou art My beloved Son in whom I am well pleased." It was not sufficient for John to know the *outer* story of his and Jesus' births, any more than it was sufficient for Jesus to know it . . . or all that the Scripture said about the prophesied Messiah. But from the moment of the coming of the dove and the word from heaven affirming His consciousness of who He was, from then on He both knew and acted as the prophesied Christ.

Do we see the point? Man, being spirit, can only operate as who he is when he has the inner spirit-knowing imparted to him. For Jesus to know and declare that He, this carpenter's son, is God's own eternal Son and the world's only hope and Savior—that is the commitment and persistence of faith. As Kierkegaard said, "That is walking on sixty-thousand fathoms of water."

What a commitment! He is to found an eternal kingdom to embrace the human race, a kingdom which has nothing to do with the founding of a kingdom of this world with its pomp and power and material display. His is to be a kingdom of the Spirit, not of this world, a kingdom whose major characteristic and activity is love—something unheard of all through the centuries and totally the opposite of all human blueprints for the occupant of David's throne. And His calling is to walk it by faith—to be the author and firstborn of the *new race*! What an adventure of faith!

Therefore, *who Jesus was* had first to be fully confirmed and demonstrated by a total confrontation with the god of self-centeredness, the god of self-interested self, this prince of the world who had already deceived and made captive the whole human race. In those forty desperate days of confrontation, the temptation was marvelously subtle. (I know of no one who has defined it more fully than did Dostoevsky, in his Legend of the Grand Inquisitor in the *The Brothers Karamazov,* with the words put in the mouth of the atheist Ivan Karamazov.) It had nothing to do with fleshly enticements. It was altogether suited to the human person who was now affirming that He was the Son of God. "If you are such," Satan says to Him, "you are the ultimate human self... with ultimate powers. Now use them for the full purpose of being a *real* human self—to own and control and manipulate all the rest of the human family for your own personal benefit."

It is in this focus that we understand the three temptations. First, if Jesus had power to make bread out of stones, He was obviously able to provide for the physical needs of all men (as He later proved He could, in feeding the five thousand). Second, if Jesus were to jump from the pinnacle of the temple and descend in safety among the crowds below, He could quickly be acclaimed as their Messiah—not because of what kind of person He was, but by appealing to their idolatrous human desire for a "superman." And third, by accepting Satan's shortcut to power, Jesus could have the kingdoms of this world to use for His own ends. Here is the history of all man's dictatorships—the masses are for the benefit of the few. Here is total self-magnification and self-gratification.

This is what the devil offered and pressed on Jesus all those forty days. "You are the superman. You *must be* if you are the Son of God. Now have the whole race at your disposal and for your own benefit. They are like a flock of sheep or a herd of cattle. They *need* a leader, so you will be benefiting them as well. Here are your three ways of doing it: Feed their bellies. Be to them the leader who captures their imagination and adoration. And use them for your own ends." This constituted the ultimate form of self-deification, and what looked like the easiest and most pleasant way to achieve it.

But Jesus was His Father's *Son*, and no usurper of His Father's prerogatives for His own ends. And His Father is the *Servant* of His creation: self-giving, not self-getting. The Son, filled with the Spirit of the Father, was likewise. So He turned back Satan's temptations—the same basic temptations as in the Garden of Eden—by quoting the outer word, "It is written," "It is written," "It is written," and equating His innermost fixed purpose with the will of His Father, whose nature is eternal, self-giving love.

So the Messiah, who by His anointing already had the inner confirmation of who He was, was now *established* as who He was by His rejection of this supreme temptation to be a self for self. It was His inner personal death and resurrection which now established Him in His freedom to later physically die and rise for a world. Not the world for Him but He for the world. This is precisely the way all we commissioned-ones have the revelation of *our own* inner union confirmed—through testings which fix us in it.

Then Jesus took the inaugural step—a public declaration at Nazareth that He was the promised One. He quoted from Isaiah regarding the prophetic nature of the coming Christ—not as an enthroned king, but a ministering servant: "The Spirit of the Lord is upon Me . . . to preach the gospel to the poor, and bring deliverance to the captives, brokenhearted, blind, and bound. And this is I. This day is this scripture fulfilled in your ears." What a statement!

What a shock to hear these words from the lips of a common carpenter!

From then on, as I read John's Gospel, I find Jesus had only one answer to every challenge and every need: *I am. I am. I am*—the light, bread, water, good shepherd, way, truth, life, the Son of the Father. This is what strikes me in John's Gospel: no profound theological explanations, but again and again *I am, I am, I am*. Yet when the secret is opened up to inquirers, "It is I, yet it is not I. I am nothing by Myself. I am saying and doing what the Father says and does in Me. It is He, not I; and yet it is I. *I am, I am.*

And He never wavered, never watered down that potent statement. No, no. It was even "Before Abraham was, *I am.* And all He was was *love, love, love*, ministered without respect of persons to all needs: yet love which ruthlessly exposed false love—the type of self-love He Himself had rejected in the temptation. So at a price that cost Him His life, while loving and never condemning anyone in need, particularly the sinners, He hated and exposed anything which masqueraded as an expression of His Father in the form of self-love or self-gain or self-glorification. Sinners He loved. Hypocrites He exposed; and above all, those who concealed their hypocrisy under the guise of representing God.

But what I am watching is not so much His words and actions, but His attitude toward Himself. He never compromised about Himself. He *was* who He *was*, the Father in the Son form, and all He came to be and do was to bring us lost humans back to that One—His Father, represented by Himself. *He alone* could do it—not doctrines, not forms of worship, not activities, but *He*—the Way, Truth, and Life.

And I am watching how *we* now, as "I ams,"* are steadfast and boldly uncompromising about ourselves as expressions of Himself. "If you see Me, you see the Father." Likewise, if you see us, you see Jesus. Never, from His baptism onward, did He say anything less than that. And then He came to the final leap of faith. He was the last Adam, the quickening Spirit. He was founding the eternal kingdom: not of this world, but a spirit family, all forms of Him. He was that Himself: the Spirit in His human, Jesus form. This meant—and He knew it from Scripture—that He must physically die, and that He would physically rise to found the new kingdom of the Spirit.

Then the last leap of faith: that this same Spirit, through His death and resurrection, would enter His followers, and they become what He was—they, common humans, become the anointed sons of God, as gods and forms of the God who is love. So He had to yield Himself up to death, and walk this way by the same faith as He had walked those three years as the I AM: believing that He would rise from the dead by the Spirit raising Him up, and that when He returned to His Father in the spirit kingdom this same Spirit would take possession of the world of humans . . . and these would form the kingdom of God.

And now, why do I enter in such detail with our Christ of history? Because *we are "I ams" also.* As He is, so are we in this world. It has meant watching Him grow from His outer understanding of Scripture and

---

*Not, of course, meaning that we are self-existent or eternal. Such is true only of the Trinity.

what He must have learned from His mother into a fixed consciousness that He is that One; His being established as who He is by Satan's temptations; His three years of constant declaration, "I am, I am, I am *He*"; and right through to His time of death, when His final confirmation before Pilate of being God's Son sent Him to the cross.

Now with *our* fixed inner consciousness, our inner baptism, *we too know*. But only by Scripture inwardly confirmed. That is all. And we are to be as uncompromising as He in saying who we are. That is why I named this book YES, I AM.

We know the reason so many hesitate to say it: It is because we haven't got it clear that our human selves are nothing but containers. As long as we wrongly think there is something in our humanity to be changed, we hesitate to say "I am." But once it becomes clear to us that we have not changed, but that *the false god is replaced by the living God,* we see we are an exchanged "I am." I was Satan in my human form, now I am Christ in my human form. And as the boldness of Jesus' positive "I am" left an indelible impression on His hearers, so it is with the boldness with which we say "I am the branch form of the Vine," "I am a body form of the Head," "I am the wife that bears the children of my heavenly Husband." Therefore *all that He is* is expressed by me—power, wisdom, love. His "I am" is my "I am."

And the hesitation of us Christians to affirm our "I am," and our tendency to self-depreciation, constantly weakens the total position which was His strength and impact, for it really means that we're not sure that we really are nothing, and He everything, and now we are everything, precisely as it was between Him and His Father.

And as with Him, so with us. We now lay down *our lives,* knowing who we are, so that others may find out who they are. We can't help it. The Intercessor has laid hold of us as we have moved on from Spirit-baptism to Spirit-intercession. That is our total occupation. We *are* this, and the Savior-Spirit in us causes us to walk in these saving ways. So we are bond-slaves of Jesus Christ. And I hope that the revelation which God has made plain to us by His Word and Spirit will bring many into that same inner confirmation which He has confirmed to us: that we are among those pressing on in our high calling as intercessors, of whom it is being said, as of The Intercessor, that "it pleased the Lord to bruise Him"; and that we say like Paul, "I bear in my body the marks of the Lord Jesus," with this one perfect outcome—"So death worketh in us, and life in you." What a life! Christ magnified in our bodies, whether by life or by death—from grace to grace, from faith to faith, from glory to glory.

Epilogue

This is the Reality

I include as a final word a letter I have just received. It is from a brother in Christ, thirty-two years of age, who lives with his wife and small son on some acres of land, which he is farming part time, in Hawaii. He also has daily employment with a construction firm as an operating engineer of heavy equipment.

I first met him over a year ago, and the letter he then sent me of the Lord's liberating revelation in him made me wonder whether I should include it in this book. But now, a year later and after another visit, this much fuller letter has come. He is, praise God, only saying what very many among God's people are saying and rejoicing in, and I hope this will become the same revelation of the Holy Spirit in many who read this book.

July, 1980

Dear Brother Norman,

Thank you very much for making yourself available to come and stay with us. We so appreciated your fellowship and your showing us the way of God more perfectly.

Every day is such a wonderful experience in

unbroken fellowship and communion with the Father. That was how He meant it to be from the beginning. I know that I am one with Him, and that I am no longer I, but Christ living in me, in my human form. And the thrilling thing is that I can do absolutely nothing to deserve or merit Him. I used to think that the Christian life was wrapped up in rules and regulations, dos and don'ts, laws and commandments, and daily disciplines. That's religion—man's way of being one with Him. I've discovered that on the cross He said, "It is finished." He settled it forever, once and for all! I am complete in Him by virtue of Him in me and as me. There is absolutely nothing I can do to add to the righteousness of God in my life. Everything that Christ is, I am—justified, sanctified, glorified, etc. (Rom. 8:30, 1 Cor. 1:2). Oh, what a wonderful mystery! One with the Father! So many know only the saving knowledge of Christ by His blood for the forgiveness of sins, and so very few know the replaced life through His resurrected and ascended body, of victory, joy, peace, overcoming, triumph, and complete rest. It is now my everyday continual experience that in fact I am a new creature, where old things are passed away and all things are become new. God intended only for His life to be manifested in us. Satan no longer has any foothold in me and sin no more power, no more dominion over me. Condemnation is a thing of the past that no longer plagues me. In reality, our becoming born-again puts us in the same standing with God the Father as Jesus being born of a virgin!

As I know who I really am, there is only victory in Christ. When trials and afflictions come, it's only God putting His Christ through such circumstances in life to bring forth life in others. I have been bought with a price ... His precious blood, and am no longer my own. I am now for others. I am now the express image of the very nature and character of God in the earth. It is written that God has "created all things for His pleasure." At first thought that sounds selfish, until one realizes that His pleasure is that of giving His all. He's not looking for something to get from us to fulfill His desires or to please Himself, but rather His pleasure is to give. That has now become my pleasure and purpose in life. I no longer look to God for what I can get out of Him for me. My nature is now His and that is to give. Now as I give, it's with the understanding that He first gave to me. He is my source. "I love Him because He first loved me."

With that in mind, trials and afflictions are a pleasure because they are for the benefit of others. I used to think trials and afflictions were the "dealings of God" to perfect *me*, to sanctify *me*, to improve *me*— me, me, me. But I've discovered that Jesus completed the work of redemption, sanctification, and perfection: "He hath [past tense] perfected forever them that are sanctified." God is no longer interested in dealing with me, but that the world through me might be saved. As long as we think trials and afflictions are for us as the dealings of God, we will forever be trying to get our lives in order and disciplined in order to reach that unobtainable goal of perfected self. We become very self-centered, self-assessing, self-disciplined. I've given up once and for all that self-assessing life, realizing the finished work He has done.

When Jesus said, "Be ye perfect, even as your Father ... ," He did not set an impossible standard for us. He accomplished the work of perfection at Calvary and it is found only in the replaced life. It is actually possible to fulfill all of Matthew 5, 6, 7 without even trying. It is possible to live a life free of sin. "As He is, so are we in this world." How can I say He *hath* perfected Me? Because it is no longer I that live, but Christ!

When we can welcome and embrace circumstances joyfully and with thanksgiving, we can endure all things and become (as you have well put it, Brother Norman), co-saviors with Christ. I am now crucified to the world and the world to me that the world I come in daily contact with might be saved. I die daily for the benefit of others, that life might spring forth in them. God has ordained difficulties and seemingly evil circumstances to happen to us for the express purpose of Christ being made manifest to others.

Knowing these things, the life of God becomes reality. We live by faith, not by sight, nor by feeling or circumstances. We live by that which is eternal and unseen, not by the physical, lying vanities around us. We are blessed with all spiritual blessings in heavenly places. This world is no longer our home. We are simply pilgrims passing through. The world of faith becomes more real to us than the physical world that we see and touch and smell and taste and hear, with our five senses. Faith establishes the word of God as fact, as evidence, as substance, as already accomplished. The promises of God are in Him "yea," and in Him "Amen"—*by us*! All we do is say "Yes" and "Amen" to what God has already said, and it is so! When we live by faith, it doesn't matter what happens around us. We no longer judge things by outward appearance, but we judge righteously. This is where life becomes fun and exciting and full of victory as we let God be the judge in life, and we live by the unseen, eternal reality!

As life becomes a walk of faith, we then see everything with a "single eye." Jesus said our eye is either single or evil. One or the other. To see double is to see evil. Adam and Eve partook of the tree of the knowledge of good and evil. They then saw with double vision. They then became judges in life rather than leaving that to God. The devil very subtly fooled them by saying, "You shall become *as* gods, knowing good and evil," when in fact the Father wanted them to *be* gods. We are always trying to *become* something when in fact we are simply to *be* the "I am" within us. It's so simple that it's complex! When we look at everything in life as good or evil, we become the judges (*as* God), always classifying everything in one category or another. We become bitter, frustrated, judgmental in life. There is no joy, no peace, no rest.

To see with a single eye is to have a pure heart. That's why Jesus said, "Blessed are the *pure* in heart, for they shall see God." Paul also speaks of living our lives in "singleness of heart." When we have a pure heart, walking in singleness of heart, with a single eye, we see only God in everything. Every circumstance, every problem, trial, affliction, seemingly evil thing, is the manifestation of God to us. We can flow with and be in harmony with everything that takes place, and be at peace with God and every man. Proverbs says, "There shall no evil happen to the just." Knowing this, life is exciting! It is fun! When we see God only in life, we can truly give thanks in and for everything!

There is such an emphasis today on getting and

keeping "the presence of God" in one's life. I also once strived and struggled and cried out to God through daily disciplines to get the "manifested presence" of God. I thought the presence of God was dependent upon what I *did*. I have since thrown all of that out of the window forever, realizing now that I in fact am the presence of God, the Holy of Holies, the temple of the Holy Ghost. I no longer have to go running around striving to get His presence in my life. *I* am the manifested presence of God, even as Jesus was upon earth in His flesh. I am the will of God in the earth, that the world through me might be saved by virtue of Him that dwells permanently within me. As Christ is lifted up, He will draw all men unto Himself—by us.

Psalm 22:3 says, "But Thou art holy, O Thou that inhabitest the praises of Israel." I've always thought that the way to get His presence was to praise Him and then He would come down and inhabit my praise and manifest Himself to me. But that's the God of the Old Covenant, the God of "influence," or as the world calls it, a philosophy. Most people look at God as an "influence": "Here I am down here, and there You are, God, up there; and if I do certain things and fulfill certain principles, You'll come down with Your presence and bless me." Even the world lives by that philosophy, feeling they'll be blessed by doing and fulfilling certain principles in life. Israel, an unregenerate people, lived by that principle. But because God is self-giving, He doesn't expect anything out of us. I don't have to fulfill anything to get His presence. My God is not a God of influence, but He's a God that has taken permanent residence. He has taken permanent abode in me. The veil was rent once and for all from the top to the bottom, opening the way into the Holy of Holies whereby I freely partake of His presence... no strings attached. Because of that, praise is now a natural, free, flowing, continual expression unto Him. Praise becomes as natural as breathing, and is a state of being and not an act. Our lives can simply *be* a praise to Him (Eph. 1:12). The act of vocal and demonstrative praise simply flows out of that state of being in which I find myself—that of union with Him, one and the same with Him. I no longer know a God coming and going, a life of ups and downs according to whether I praise Him or not. There is such a higher realm where He becomes you and you become Him and are one with the Father.

The organized church today is, by and large, a modern Moses' Tabernacle, trying to fulfill certain principles, rules and regulations, dos and don'ts, laws and commandments, and daily disciplines in order to get the presence and approval of God. That's fine, as long as one does *all* that; but Scripture says that no one can keep the law. It also says that whoever does the law must also live in it. You're blessed if you can do it, but cursed if you can't. (I've been trying for thirteen years, but never could.) Besides that, even if one could keep all the principles, laws, disciplines, etc., there is room for pride saying, "I've done it." But God will share His glory with no man. There is absolutely nothing we can do to merit His presence or approval; neither does God expect us to do anything to obtain it, because of His very self-giving nature.

It is the tangible, felt, manifested presence of God that the organized church is looking for today. They'll never find it though, and only become frustrated in the process, because Jesus said, "The kingdom of God cometh not with observation, but behold, the kingdom of God is within you." It is a wicked and adulterous generation that seeketh for a sign, a manifestation of God. Once again, the signs and manifestations will automatically and naturally follow them that believe. It will be a natural outflow of who we are and not what we do.

For years I have been asking God for a great hunger and thirst for Him. I felt that the more hunger and thirst I had, the more God would come to me. I now realize I've been wasting my time and energy. But as I now understand who He is within me, I am full, I am satisfied, my thirst is quenched, my hunger is gone. Even as the Scriptures declare, out of my belly, my innermost being, flow rivers of living water. Jesus said, "He that drinks of the water that I shall give him shall never thirst." He said, "Blessed are they that hunger and thirst after righteousness, for they shall be filled." He also said, "He that cometh to *Me* shall never hunger; and he that believeth on *Me* shall never thirst." *There is an end!* That end is Christ! I no longer hunger or thirst. I now only know a permanently satisfied, fulfilled life in Christ—full and overflowing for the benefits of others.

I've given up trying to improve my life. All I have to do is to be who I really am, which is Christ in me. If I may be so bold, I am a god, created in His very image with the indwelling Christ my all. It's no longer I that live, yet it is I, yet not I, but Christ. No wonder Paul calls it a mystery! Jesus was the firstborn among many brethren. He came as a Son to be an intercessor to bring many sons to glory. Paul said, "Let this mind be in you which was also in Christ

Jesus," the "mind" of total self-emptying, and then spoke of Jesus' exaltation. I, too, am to have this intercessory mind of total self-emptying to take humanity's lowest place on the cross. And any exaltation that follows will be from God.

After years of struggling and striving, frustration and failure (a necessary step!), I have finally ceased from my own works and entered into rest. Oh, what fellowship divine, what communion, what rest! I know Him, even as I am known of Him. I used to work so hard at being a Christian . . . and, as a result, God was at rest. Now I'm at rest and He's at work! In this rest, prayer becomes a state of being. It's no longer an act of formality. It's continual communion and fellowship with the Father. Then and only then is it possible to fulfill the scripture "Pray without ceasing."

I have come to a realization that it was not *I* that committed myself to *Him*. It was *He* that committed Himself to *me*. My spiritual life is dependent upon His total commitment to me. As long as I think that my walk with God depends upon my decision, my dedication, my commitment to Him, then life becomes a never-ending parade of recommitment, rededication, reconsecretion to Him. In reality, however, the Christian life is dependent on replacement.

Hallelujah, it is wonderful in Him! The best Bible college there is is life itself! "For me to live is Christ." Our mission on earth is to live and to be the Christ to an unregenerate world around us.

I have concluded in my life that it is absolutely impossible to live the Christian life, and that God never intended us to do so. He intended the Christ within us to live it. Then and only then is it possible to fulfill the law and the spirit of the law (Matt. 5, 6, 7). And it only comes as a revelation from the Father. Jesus asked Peter, "Who do you say that I am?" Peter said, "Thou art the Christ." Jesus told him, "Flesh and blood hath not revealed it unto thee, but My Father which is in heaven." Jesus then told Peter, "Upon this rock [upon this foundation, upon this revelation] I will build My church." Paul said that "the gospel which was preached of me is not after man. For I neither received it of man, neither was I taught it, but by the revelation of Jesus Christ." Many try to build the church upon principles, upon teachings, upon everything imaginable except the Christ. But "except the Lord build the house, they that build it labor in vain." It is upon this revelation of the Christ that life is fun. Life is exciting, fulfilling, and wonderful. Oh what fellowship, what communion, what victory! Hallelujah to Him for ever!

I'm sure I'm repeating to you many things that you've already grasped years ago. But I appreciate your listening ear . . . to be able to repeat these things to you as they are revealed to me. I love you, Brother Norman. Thank you for your love and rich fellowship.

One with Him and you,
(Signed) Christopher Bernard

If The Lord Says I Am, Yes, I Am

(We sometimes sing this little song—no great poetry, not set to great music, but great truth. Alongside each phrase, I list the Bible statement.)

	Acts 11:26
If the Lord says I'm a Christian, yes, I am,	2 Cor. 5:17
If the Lord says I'm made new, yes, I am,	1 Cor. 6:17
If the Lord says I'm one spirit with Himself,	
If the Lord says I am, yes, I am.	
	1 John 3:2
If the Lord says I'm a son, yes, I am,	Rom. 8:17
If the Lord says I'm an heir, yes, I am,	
If the Lord says I'm a citizen of His kingdom here and now,	Eph. 2:19
If the Lord says I am, yes, I am.	
	2 Cor. 4:7
If the Lord says I'm a vessel, yes, I am,	John 15:5
If the Lord says I'm a branch, yes, I am,	
If the Lord says I'm a temple of His Holy Spirit in me,	1 Cor. 6:19
If the Lord says I am, yes, I am.	
	1 Cor. 1:2
If the Lord says I'm a saint, yes, I am	2 Tim. 2:10
If the Lord says I'm elect, yes, I am	
If the Lord says I'm a partaker of His divine nature,	2 Pet. 1:4
If the Lord says I am yes, I am.	
	Rev. 1:6
If the Lord says I'm a priest, yes, I am,	Rev. 1:6
If the Lord says I'm a king, yes, I am,	
If the Lord says I am seated in the heavenly places in Christ,	Eph. 2:6

This is the Reality

If the Lord says I am, yes, I am.
                                                    Eph. 1:4
If the Lord says I am holy, yes, I am,
If the Lord says I am blameless, yes,   Eph. 1:4
    I am,
If the Lord says I am unreprovable   Col. 1:22
    in His sight,
If the Lord says I am, yes, I am.
                                                    Col. 2:10
If the Lord says I'm complete, yes, I am,   Phil. 3:15
If the Lord says I am perfect, yes, I am,
If the Lord says that I am as He is in   1 John 4:17
    this world,
If the Lord says I am, yes, I am.
                                                    1 Cor. 4:8
If the Lord says I am filled, yes, I am,   1 John 2:14
If the Lord says I am strong, yes, I am,
If the Lord says I am more than   Rom. 8:37
    conqueror in this world,
If the Lord says I am, yes, I am.

If the Lord says I'm not I but He in me,   Gal. 2:20
    yes, I am,
If the Lord says I'm the world's light,   Matt. 5:14
    yes, I am,
If the Lord says I'm a god to whom His   John 10:34-35
    word has come,
If the Lord says I am, yes, I am.